# Cricut Explore Air 2

Complete Beginners Guide to Use The
Cricut Explore Air 2, Master Cricut
Design Space, And Craft out Creative
Project Ideas

## Tiffany Nicholas

## Disclaimer

All the information contained in this book is purely for educational activities only. The writer does not assert the accuracy or wholesomeness of any info gotten from this book. The views contained within the pages of this material are those of the author in its entirety. The author/writer will not be held accountable or liable for any missing information, omissions or errors, damages, injuries, or any loses that may occur from the use of information gotten form this book.

## Dedication

This guide is dedicated to the lovers of homemade cutting crafts.

# TABLE OF CONTENTS

# INTRODUCTION

The first time I set my eyes on Cricut Explore Air 2, what beat me is its slick design. The design section of the Cricut incorporations is doing a great job when it comes to the awesomeness of their products. I'm always impressed with the way the machines opens. Its door will open with a bit of delay. There is no way you won't like seen such movement.

Another unique thing about this Cricut machine is that the tools that come with it are made from high-quality materials and have two cutting modes- Normal and fast modes that will afford you having precision projects.

The Cricut Explore Air 2 is designed to cut different kinds of materials that include fabrics, cardstock, paper, poster board, iron-on, faux leather, vellum, canvas, aluminum foil, washi sheet, magnetic cloth, etc.

Before this Cricut Explore Air 2, the company has created Cricut machines that made them famous. Earlier they have created Cricut Explore One, Cricut Explore Air, and Cricut

Explore Air 2.

**Why Cricut Explore Air 2?**

Cricut Explore Air 2 is designed to be a small die-cutting machine that will work twice faster in speed than other older Cricut machine. So to crafters who work on mass production, 2x advantage of this cutting machine is just what the crafter is looking for to enhance her productivity.

Cricut Explore Air 2 comes with the dual carriage, meaning that you have the liberty of using two tools at the same time with this machine. There are two clamps: A and B. A is for the Accessories like scoring stylus and pen, while B is for cutting Blade.

When considering this fantastic machine's size and weight, it has a decent size and significant weight attached to it. Though it is recommended to have a designated spot to place your Cricut, with Cricut Explore Air 2, you may just have to set aside a place so to avoid moving it left and right.

It's not surprising that most brands have their software. But for Cricut, the software that guides its operations is known as Cricut Design Space. This is online software that comes with many benefits. With Design Space, you don't need the installation of any other software. Download it and begin your crafting. Another use of this software is that it works on any internet compliant device once they are compatible.

The Design Space is cloud-based, so you need the internet to access it, and if you have a slow internet connection, you will not be able to access it.

With the Design Space nature, you can launch it on smart devices, such as tablets, smartphones, and computers. You can use the above tools to craft your design, and it can be printed and cut by Cricut Explore Air 2. Remember that you can start a design on one of the above devices and finish it on another device with no problem. You can now see how flexible is designing a project will be. It can be done on a bus, taxi, canteen, metro with your mobile device, and at home using your laptop.

Every other detail that will make you see why you did not make a mistake in buying this machine is discussed in this guide.

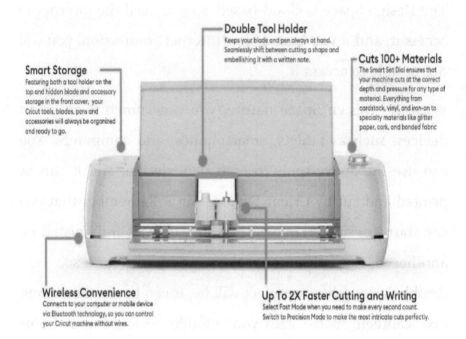

**Smart Storage**
Featuring both a tool holder on the top and hidden blade and accessory storage in the front cover, your Cricut tools, blades, pens and accessories will always be organized and ready to go.

**Double Tool Holder**
Keeps your blade and pen always at hand. Seamlessly shift between cutting a shape and embellishing it with a written note.

**Cuts 100+ Materials**
The Smart Set Dial ensures that your machine cuts at the correct depth and pressure for any type of material. Everything from cardstock, vinyl, and iron-on to specialty materials like glitter paper, cork, and bonded fabric

**Wireless Convenience**
Connects to your computer or mobile device via Bluetooth technology, so you can control your Cricut machine without wires.

**Up To 2X Faster Cutting and Writing**
Select Fast Mode when you need to make every second count. Switch to Precision Mode to make the most intricate cuts perfectly.

**Chapter 1.**

# CRICUT EXPLORE AIR 2

## CRICUT EXPLORE AIR 2 AND USEFULNESS

The Cricut Explore Air 2 is a chance to make your possibilities limitless. Cricut Explore Air 2 is the fastest Cricut machine. It can be used to create personalized items, create excellent looking homemade projects, cut, write and score professional designs faster than you could ever think.

This tech is fantastic as it is two times faster than the earlier Cricut Explore. It has the ability to cut 100+ materials, from cardstocks, leather, paper, to vellum. With its Smart set dial and ability to choose Custom Material in the Design Space environment, you will be able to have control of over 100 various material settings.

The Cricut Explore Air 2 comes with the ability to cut wirelessly and offers to score with the built-in Bluetooth.

With this machine's introduction to the Cricut family, you will have the chance to cut delicate details with precision to get beautiful and excellent decor details. Its Cricut Pens can be used to create handwritten projects, with 370+ fonts to select from, or the chance to use your preferred fonts from your devices (computer/ Mobile). Remember also that with Cricut Explore Air 2, you will be able to create a great, perfect fold line for cards, 3D papercrafts, boxes, and many more with the Scoring Stylus.

With Cricut Explore Air 2 in conjunction with the Design Space, you will have access to more than 60 000 images in the Cricut Image Library that can be used for design in computers (Windows/Mac) and mobile devices (iOS/Android). You have the liberty to transform the images in your projects to anything you imagined, turn into realities, and design with an internet connection.

Other Benefits of Cricut Explore Air 2:

• It gives iOS the advantage of offline mode.

• You can upload your image free when using this machine (.jpg, .gif, .svg, .bmp, .dxf, .png).

• Cricut Explore Air 2 is straight forward to use.

• It works with Cricut cartridges.

• It will cut printable images.

• Cricut Explore Air 2 comes with the dual carriage for cutting and writing.

• It also comes with a dual carriage for cutting and scoring in an easy step.

• It also has integrated storage compartments.

• It can be connected to Design Space with the aid of Bluetooth to achieve wireless cutting.

## UNBOXING EXPLORE AIR 2 AND ITS FEATURES

The Cricut Explore Air 2 originally comes with Black, Mint, Raspberry, Lilac, Gold, Fuschia, Rose, and Blue. Other Colors such as Cobalt, Boysenberry, Merlot, Peacock, Persimmon, and Sunflower are available in some retailers.

The Cricut Explore Air 2 comes in a packaged that housed Cricut Explore Air2 machine, the adapter, let's get started pack (user's guide and instructions), cord extension, USB cord, and a pen. Depending on what you purchased, it may be Cricut Explore with Essential Bundle or With Everything Bundle. But ordinarily, you should have a cardstock sample and a 12 x 12-inch LightGrip cutting mat, and carbide premium blade (preassembled).

**Before Opening**

**After Opening**

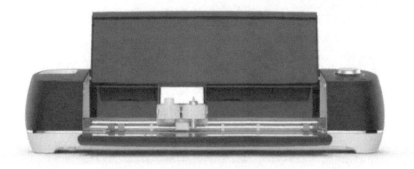

## Look Inside

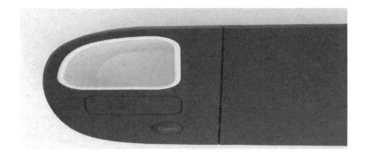

## Open Button and Save Box

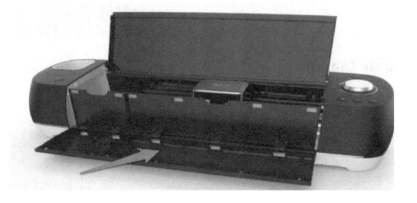

## Down save Box

**Controller and On Button**

**Double Clamps**

**Pen**

**Carbide Blade**

**Cardstock**

**Mat 12 x 12**

## Features:

### Dimensions and Weight:

Dimensions: 5.97" (151.59mm) x 22.17" (563.3mm) x 6.99" (177.57mm)

Weight: 9.6kg (21 lbs.)

**Bluetooth:**

Cricut Explore Air 2 comes with in-built Bluetooth that allows you to connect the machine wirelessly to your computer or your mobile device via the Cricut app. Regardless of the inbuilt Bluetooth, Cricut Explore Air 2 also comes with a USB cord to help connect to the computer if that's the way you preferred. How to pair your machine with your device will be discussed in chapter 2 on how to set up your machine. However, remember that whenever you want to connect the setup for the first time, it will ask for a pin; don't be disturbed as the Cricut pin is 0000. The moment it is connected, the power button will turn blue.

**Double clamps:**

Your Cricut Explore Air 2 comes with two clamps for holding tools and blades. The clamps are lettered A and B. Clamp A is used to hold pens or accessories or scoring stylus, while clamp B is to hold the blade. With this arrangement, you have the chance to send a project to be drawn and then be cut without having to change the blade and pen. However, if you want to use multiple colors of pens, or the intended project require scoring and pen drawing, you will have to switch them. Note the Design Space will let you know which of the tools will draw or score next, to see the tool to put into the clamp.

**Blade options:**

With Cricut Explore Air 2, you have the chance of using different kinds of the blade; fine point fabric housing (to cut bonded fabrics), and deep cut.

**What types of materials can Cricut Explore Air 2 cut?**

Once you select your machine on the Design Space environment, there will be a dropdown of the materials that your machine is capable of cutting. The materials included that the Cricut Explore Air2 can cut include stencil material, acetate, washi paper, thin balsa wood, vinyl, faux leather, cardstock, iron-on, paper, etc.

**Others:**

• Comparable with Design Space software for Windows, Mac, Android, and iOS.

• Comes with more than 100 free images and 50 projects

• Compatible with Cricut cartridges.

• You can upload and make use of your images and fonts.

## ACCESSORIES OF THE CRICUT EXPLORE AIR 2

You have successfully purchased your Cricut Explore Air 2, and you are thinking of the best tools and accessories that will compliment your machine. Some retailers are selling these tools and accessories as a bundle with the machine; some sell with the essential bundle, and some sell with everything bundle. Though the price differs but the advantage of Everything Bundle is for those buying Cricut machine for the first time. But to those who have been using other models, it is unnecessary to purchase tools that you have unless they are wrong. But you may need to buy more accessories as it may affect the projects you want to work on.

So below are some of the must-have accessories and tools;

**Cutting Weed tool:**

Cricut weeding tool is used to remove the tiny unwanted pieces of the cut out material. It can also be used to pick items that have adhesive on it.

## Cutting Weed tool

## Cricut Infusible Ink Pens:

With these pens, you can create designs that can be placed on blank items like coasters, bags, t-shirts, water bottles, etc. These infusible inks so adhere to the blank item very well that there will not be stiff lines or fraying edges around the designs, as if it just like an iron-on transfer. They come in different kinds of colors that are rich and vibrant.

## Cricut Infusible Ink Pens

## Cricut Standard Grip Adhesive Cutting Mats:

As its name implies, it is used to aid your cutting on the Cricut machine. All the Cricut machines, including the newest model Cricut Joy, make use of cutting mats. You are expected to choose the right mat for the kind of project you are doing. Note that some mats are for cardstock or fabric.

**Cricut Standard Grip Adhesive Cutting Mats**

## Cricut Scoring Stylus:

This tool is used in Cricut Explore Air 2 to score lines, especially when creating a project that you intend to fold, such as 3D craft or greeting card.

**Cricut Scoring Stylus**

**Cricut Scraper:**

Your Cricut scraper will help you in cleaning up your work by scooping up tiny scraps of materials without hassle. This scraper can also be used to make your vinyl bubble-free. Cricut scraper comes in various sizes. The image below is XL Scrapper.

**Cricut XL Scraper**

**Cricut Brayer:**

This handy tool helps to stick materials such as vinyl or fabric to mats entirely flat to prevent bubbles and wrinkles that may want to ruin your projects. Press the Brayer on the material placed on the cutting mat, and it will smoothen it well and get rid of the air bubbles.

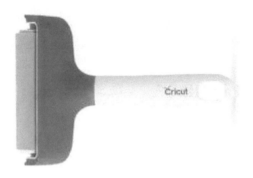

**Cricut Brayer**

**Cricut BrightPad Mint:**

This Pad is for those who find it difficult to clean out their works due to sight issues. This is a special pad that illuminates with the aid of adjustable LED light to weed and trace the papers' scores.

**Cricut BrightPad Mint**


**Cricut Explore Blade &Housing:**

## Cricut Explore Deep Cut Housing & Blade

The information below about the Cricut blades will be useful for Cricut Explore Air. The blades that can be used for Cricut Explore Air 2 fine are point series of blades and housing.

### Fine-Point Blades

The Cricut fine-point blades are designed in a way to be identified with color. With this color-coded design, it will be straightforward to know which of the blade is used for a specific material.

### Premium Fine-Point Blade: Gold

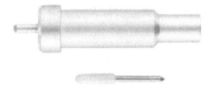

### Premium Fine-Point Blade Gold

The Premium Fine-point blades are created to cut intricate materials that are from thin to medium-weight. This type of blade is made of premium German carbide steel. This Gold type is known formerly as the Premium German Carbide blade.

**Features:**

• They are gold in color.

• Use this type for cardstock, paper, iron-on, poster board, and thin to medium-weight materials.

• This type of blade must be used with gold Premium Fine-Point Housing or silver Fine-Point Housing if it is not available.

**Deep Point Blade**

**Deep Point Blade**

22

The Deep Point Blade is another type in the family of fine point blades. This blade will afford you the best opportunity to make it easy to do intricate cuts on so many kinds of materials. This blade comes with a steeper blade angle of 60 degrees vs. 45 degrees, and they are harder and more durable.

**Features:**

• They are black.

• Suitable for thicker materials, which include chipboard, magnet, thick cardstock, stamp material, fabrics, foam sheets, stiffened felt, and cardboard.

• Use Deep-Point Housing with it.


**Bonded-Fabric Blade**

**Bonded-Fabric Blade**

To prolong your fabric-cutting life, it is recommended for you to use Cricut fabric cutters. The bonded-Point blade will allow you all the functions of the Premium Fine-Point blade.

**Features:**

• They are Pink in color.

• Great for cuts that are delicate on bonded fabrics or fabrics that come with iron-on backer.

• Use Bonded-Fabric Blade Housing with it and, if not available, use with Premium Fine-Point Blade Housing.

**Note:** Deep-Point blades should be used with Deep-Point blade housings. Also, Premium Fine-Point blades should be used with Premium Fine-Point blade housings.

**Others;**

• Scissors - with protective blade cover.

• Spatula - This is used to lift cuts from the mat.

• High-quality trimmer can be used for materials up to 12" wide.

• Replacement blade for the trimmer.

• Scoring blade (for trimmer) allows you to add score lines to your projects.

# Chapter 2

# HOW TO SETUP CRICUT EXPLORE AIR 2 MACHINE

## SETTING UP YOUR MACHINE

The first task in this business of creating crafts with the Cricut machine is the ability to complete setting up your machine and be able to register the machine automatically to your Design Space account. The steps below illustrate how to set up any of the following Cricut Machine; Explore Air, Explore One, Explore Air 2, Explore, or Maker.

**Windows/Mac**

**Steps:**

1. Insert the power cable into the round hole at the back of the machine and power it on.

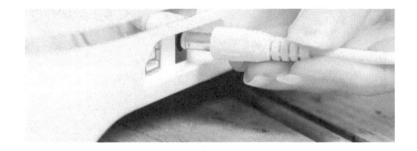

2. Attach the USB cord to the remaining hole at the back of the Cricut machine.

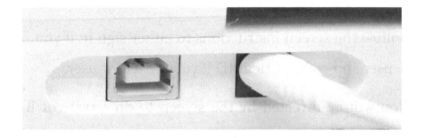

3. Then attach the other end of the USB cable to your laptop or connect the machine via Bluetooth.

4. Launch the browser on your computer and go to design.cricut.com/setup.

5. Download and install the Design Space for your desktop (check chapter 4 for details).

6. Follow the screen instructions to either sign in if you not a new user and create Cricut ID if you are a new user.

7. You will be directed by the screen to do a test cut if you successfully complete the setup.

**IOS/Android**

**Steps:**

1. Insert the power cable into the round hole at the back of the machine and power it on.

2. Pair your iOS or Android with your Cricut machine via Bluetooth.

3. Download and install the Design Space for your desktop (check chapter 4 for details).

28

4. Open the Design Space, sign in if you are not a new user, and create Cricut ID if you are a new user.

5. Click on the menu and choose Machine Setup.

6. Pick your machine from the list of your Bluetooth pair devices and follow the screen's instructions to complete your set up.

7. You will be directed by the screen to do a test cut if you successfully complete the setup.

## HOW TO PAIR CRICUT EXPLORE AIR 2 VIA BLUETOOTH

With the feature, you can cut wirelessly, making use of Cricut Maker, Explore and Joy through Bluetooth. To achieve this feat, follow the steps below to pair Cricut Machine with either a mobile device or computer.

**Windows**

Note: The following steps and screenshots are only applicable to Windows 10. To other uses of Windows OS, it is recommended to contact Member Care on the Cricut site.

**Steps:**

1. Make sure your Cricut machine is powered on, and you are 10 to 15 feet to the computer that is paired with.

2. If your computer is not Bluetooth enabled and, attach a wireless Bluetooth adapter to your computer. Not all dongle work with Cricut but get the one that can work with audio appliances.

3. To be sure your laptop is Bluetooth enabled, go to the computer screen, right-click on the Start button, and choose Device Manager.

4. If Bluetooth is among the list, it's an indication that your Bluetooth is enabled.

5. Select Device Manager.

6. Click the Start menu and choose Settings.

7. Launch the Device features.

8. Make sure that the Bluetooth is ON and select Add Bluetooth or other device.

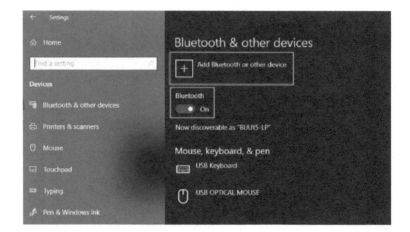

9. Choose Bluetooth and allow the computer to locate your Cricut machine. Then choose your machine from the paired list.

10. If you are asked to input a PIN, input 0000, and then choose Connect.

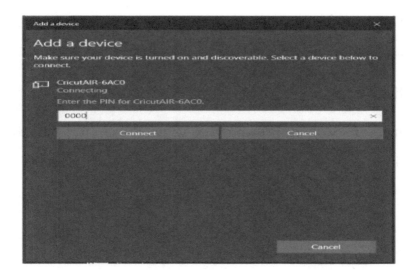

11. If you follow the above steps very well, your Cricut machine will now be paired with the computer.

## Mac

Note that it is possible for the mac computer not to show "Connected". It can only show this if the program is communicating with the machine while cutting.

## Steps:

1. Make sure your Cricut machine is powered on, and you are 10 to 15 feet to the computer that is paired with.

2. Most computers are Bluetooth enabled and, if not, attach a wireless Bluetooth adapter to your computer. Not all dongle work with Cricut but get the one that supports audio devices.

3. To check if your Mac computer is Bluetooth enabled, take these steps:

•.Click on the Apple Menu.

•.Click on System Preferences; then search for Bluetooth option.

4. Launch the Bluetooth window. If the window is off, press the button to On it. Then choose the adapter/Bluetooth name from the list.

5. Choose Pair when asking for Pin input 0000 and pick Pair.

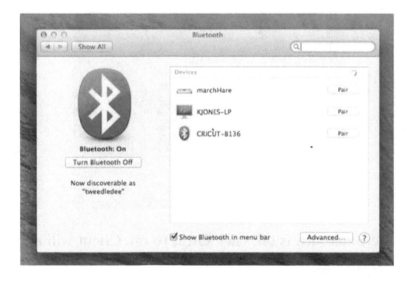

6. If you follow the above steps very well, your Cricut machine will now be paired with the computer.

## iOS

**Steps:**

1. Make sure your Cricut machine is powered on, and you are 10 to 15 feet to the mobile device that is paired with.

2. Click on Settings and later Bluetooth.

3. If the Bluetooth is off, click On it to on. Cricut will appear once the Bluetooth is on.

4. Pick the Bluetooth/Adapter name from the list.

5. When asking for Pin, input 0000, and pick Pair.

6. If you follow the above steps very well, your Cricut machine will now be paired with the mobile device.

## Android

## Steps:

1. Make sure your Cricut machine is powered on, and you are 10 to 15 feet to the mobile device that is paired with.

2. Click on Settings and later Bluetooth.

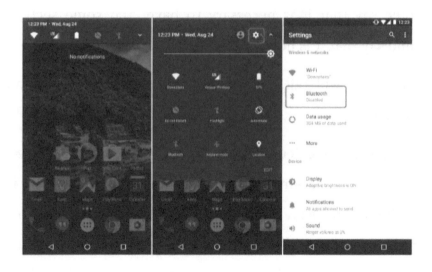

3. If the Bluetooth is off, click on it to on. Cricut will appear once the Bluetooth is on.

4. Pick the Bluetooth/Adapter name from the list.

5. When asking for Pin, input 0000, and pick Pair.

6. If you follow the above steps very well, your Cricut machine will now be paired with the mobile device.

## DIFFERENCE BETWEEN CRICUT ACCESS AND DESIGN SPACE

There is a widely wrong notion about Cricut Access, as some people say that it is necessary to have, and some sections would say that it is not.

So here we will tell you all that you need to know about Cricut Access.

Firstly, what is Cricut Access? The Cricut Access is a paid membership platform that gives instant access to its members to have an impressive library of more than 100 000 fonts, images, and ready to cut projects. There are three types of plans on Cricut Access; Monthly, Annual, and the Premium. The kind of plan that you subscribed to will depend on other accrued benefits such as discounts on licensed fonts, physical products, and images that you will get.

With the above little information, what's, is the difference between Cricut Access and design Space? Design Space is a free software where you can upload projects, design and send the final work to the Cricut machine to be cut without mincing words. The Cricut Access is a paid membership platform filled with fonts, graphics, images, and ready to be cut projects that you can use in the Design Space environment.

You can make use of all the graphics in the Cricut Access while creating your projects in the Design Space without being a paid member, but you won't be able to send the project to your Cricut machine for cutting. So my candid advice is that if you don't want to pay for the graphics, don't make use of the graphics from Cricut Access. Instead of using graphics that will not be able to come out with your final project due to cost, why can't you use graphics in the Design Space. With Design Space, you can use your own images and fonts to create your designs with freebies such as squares, circles, etc.

However, suppose you want to be using your Cricut machine often or find it very difficult to create or illustrate projects or don't know how to get free projects online. In that case, it is recommended to subscribe to Cricut Access. Cricut Access is an excellent way to cut time and to make projects right away instead of creating the design or take time to search for free projects online.

**Cricut Access Plans**

If you are a paid member, you have access to;

100,000 + graphics, images, and ready to cut projects (unlimited use).

400 + fonts (unlimited use).

10% discounts on all physical products bought on cicut.com.

10% discounts on cartridges, images, cut ready projects on a font from companies like Sesame Street, Disney, Hello Kitty, etc.

50% less wait time when calling Care Line.

**1. Monthly Plan (The perfect starter plan)**

This plan costs $9.99, and this is just you for you if you want to see why you should use Cricut Access. If you are not comfortable with the platform, you have the chance to cancel the plan since it is for just a month.

**2. Annual Plan (Big-time benefits)**

This plan costs $ 95.58 annually, and the monthly subscription is $7.99. This plan has the same benefits as that of the Perfect Starter Plan.

3. Premium Plan (The best value)

This is billed $119.88 yearly, and apart from the benefits of the previous plans, it also has more such as;

50% discounts on graphics, licensed fonts, and ready to make and cut projects. Free Economy Shipping when you order more than $50.

# HOW TO CRICUT ACCESS

**How to Purchase Cricut Access**

You have the option of purchasing Cricut Access either through Cricut.com or Cricut Design Space on your computer or mobile device (Android or iOS).

**Desktop**

## How to purchase Cricut Access monthly

**Steps:**

1. Sign in to your Design Space.

2. Choose the design Space menu and pick Cricut Access.

3. Depending on your eligibility.

If you are eligible for a free trial, you will have the option of Start My Trial.

If you have exhausted your free trial, you will have the option to purchase a Monthly or Yearly plan.

**Free trial**

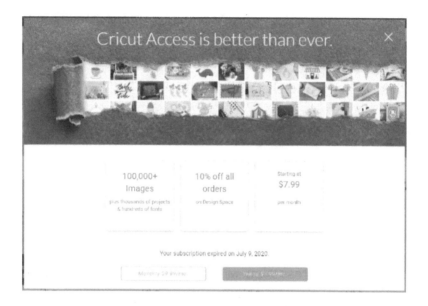

Cricut Access is better than ever. ×

100,000+
Images
plus thousands of projects
& hundreds of fonts

10% off all
orders
on Design Space

Starting at
$7.99
per month

Your subscription expired on July 9, 2020.

Monthly $9.99/mo | Yearly $9.99/mo

## Monthly or yearly Plan

4. Input your payment details, and choose Confirm. If asked, input your Cricut password to verify the purchase.

5. The Cricut Access plan will be activated instantly, and it will be available in the Design Space platforms.

## How to purchase Cricut Access Yearly

## Steps:

1. Sign in to your Design Space.

2. On your Design Space, create a new project.

3. Place an image of Cricut Access (an image that is marked with green "a").

4. Pick Make It, and then Checkout.

5. Input your payment details, and choose Continue.

6. Select the Yearly option.

7. Input the Cricut password and choose to Authorize the purchase.

8. The Cricut Access plan will be activated instantly and will be available in the Design Space platforms.

## iOS

How to purchase Cricut access via iOS

**Steps:**

1. Sign in to your Design Space.

2. Choose the Design Space menu and pick the Cricut Access.

3. Choose to Sign Me Up.

4. iTunes app will process the purchase through your account. Then choose Confirm. Input your Apple Id password and choose Sign In to confirm the purchase.

5. The Cricut Access plan will be activated instantly and available in the Design Space platforms.

## Android

How to purchase Cricut access via Android

**Steps:**

1. 1. Sign in to your Design Space.

2. Choose the Design Space menu and pick the Cricut Access.

3. Choose to Sign Me Up.

4. Recheck the item in the cart and choose Subscribe.

5. Google paly will process the purchase through your Google play account. Then choose Confirm. Input your Google play password and choose Sign In to confirm the purchase.

6. The Cricut Access plan will be activated instantly and available in the Design Space platforms.

## cricut.com

How to purchase Cricut access via Cricut.com

This option only available in the USA and Canada.

**Steps:**

1. Launch shop.cricut.com from your preferred browser.

2. Sign in to your system with the Cricut Id and password.

3. Choose and add the Cricut Access you want to the cart.

4. Continue until you complete your purchase.

5. The moments your order is completed, your Cricut Access plan will now activate and be available in the design Spaces.

## HOW TO LINK CARTRIDGES WITH CRICUT EXPLORE AIR 2

The Cricut Explore Air 2 is designed in such a way that you will not be able to use it without the internet, but you can make use of cartridges in the machine. The following steps are processes to link cartridges with your Cricut Explore Air 2.

**Steps:**

1. Connect your Cricut Explore Air 2 to the computer.

2. Launch cricut.com on your browser and sign in to your Design Space account.

3. Once you have logged in, tap the green account button and choose "Cartridge Linking" from the dropdown list.

4. Put the cartridge well into the top port on your Cricut machine.

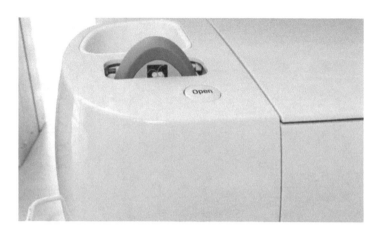

**Cartridge into port**

5. Once the cartridge is detected, you will be taken to your account, and then tap "Link Cartridge."

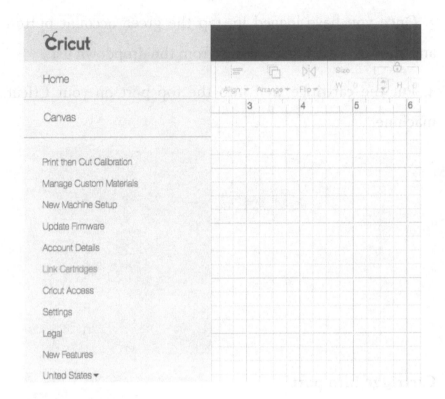

## Link Cartridge

## Tips on Cartridges

Cricut cartridge can only be linked to one Cricut account.

Once a cartridge has been linked to an account, it cannot be unlinked.

Cricut cartridge cannot be moved to another account.

Once you have linked your Cricut cartridge to your Design Space in one system, you don't need to relink it to your Design Space in another system.

You cannot use a physical Cricut cartridge with your Cricut Explore Air unless you link it with your account.

# Chapter 3

# CALIBRATION OF THE CRICUT EXPLORE AIR 2

## HOW TO CALIBRATE PRINTER FOR PRINT THEN CUT

This option of calibrating the printer for print then cut will help your Cricut Explore Air 2 cuts in precision along the images' edge to be printed. Please choose your device below to know its step by step instructions.

Note: Presently, this option is not available on android.

**Windows/Mac**

**Steps:**

1. Log into your Design Space and choose the account menu. Then select Calibration.

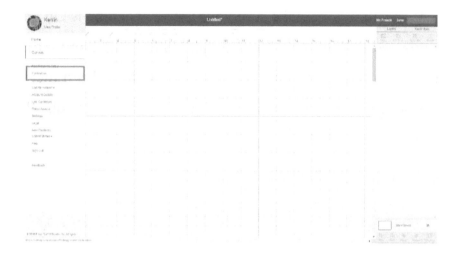

2. Choose Print Then Cut.

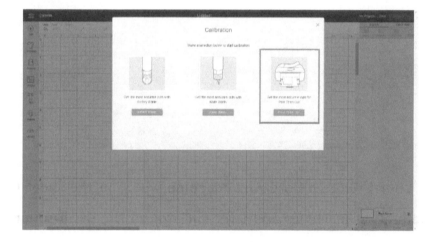

3. Choose your preferred printer and then choose Print.

4. Now, put the printed calibrated sheet on the machine mat and place it on its top left side. Choose Continue.

5. At this junction, make sure your Cricut machine is On and connected to the computer through USB or Bluetooth. From the computer, select your device from the drop-down menu, choose the material setting, and load the mat on the machine.

6. Then click the flashing Go button.

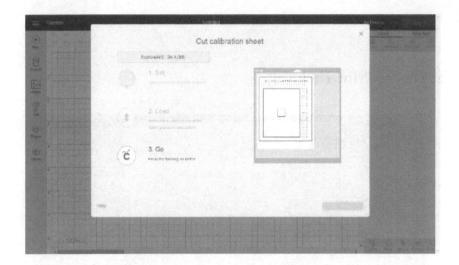

7. Your Cricut Explore Air2 machine will scan the sheet for calibration markings and later cut around the small squares near the sheet's center. Check the cut if its does it job on the printed line without unloading the mat. If it touches, choose Yes in the Design Space and choose to Continue to go to the next step.

Note: If you choose No, the Design Space will go to the next step to get closer to the line.

7b. Your Cricut Explore Air 2 will start the calibration cut on the page's top and side. Once it is done, using Without Unloading the mat, check the line along the page's top and side closely. It is possible for some not to touch the printed lines. Design Space will ask you to choose the numbers and letters cuts that are very close to the printed lines' center. Choose the Top then right-click to give a dropdown that shows the line number or letter with cuts that are very close to the line's center. Once done, choose Continue.

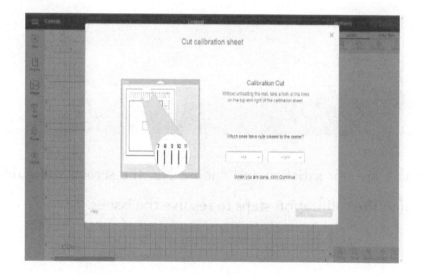

8. Your machine will now perform a confirmation cut just around the large rectangle on the sheet. When done, unload the mat, take the calibration sheet away, and answer the Design Space's final question.

If you are satisfied with the cut, choose Yes, and then Continue to the final calibration screen.

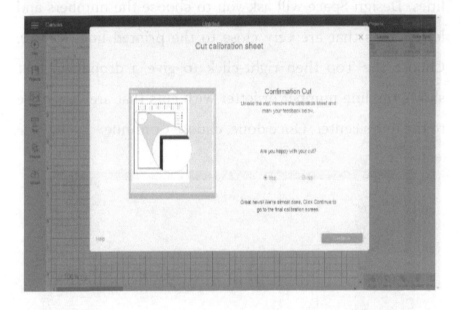

If you are not satisfied and choose No, the screen will guide you in the calibration steps to resolve the issues.

9. Choose Save & Close to save the calibration settings.

10. Now Print Then Cut.

If you still require some help with Print Then Cut, contact the Member Care.

## iOS

Note: Make sure that your Cricut Explore Air 2 is paired with your iOS mobile device.

**Steps:**

1. Sign in to your Cricut Design Space on iOS device and click on the account menu. Choose "Print Then Cut Calibration." The Print Then Cut calibration will display on your screen.

2. First, print the calibration sheet out on your home printer. Click on "Print Sheet" on the screen.

A) Using a Home Printer

Tap Print Sheet to print a calibration sheet.

Help      Print Sheet      Continue

3. Your screen will display a preview of the calibration sheet. If your home printer is not selected already, click on "Select Printer." choose your home printer from the list of options, then go back to the Printer Options screen, and click on "Print" on the screen. The calibration sheet will be printed on the home printer.

4. Next step is to put the printed calibration sheet on your cutting mat and place it on the top left side of the mat. Then click on "Continue."

5. Choose the right material setting, then load the mat into your machine, and press the flashing "Go" button.

6. Your Cricut Explore Air2 machine will scan the sheet for calibration markings and later cut around the small squares near the sheet's center. Check the cut if it does its job on the printed line without unloading the mat. If it touches, choose Yes in the Design Space and choose to Continue to go to the next step.

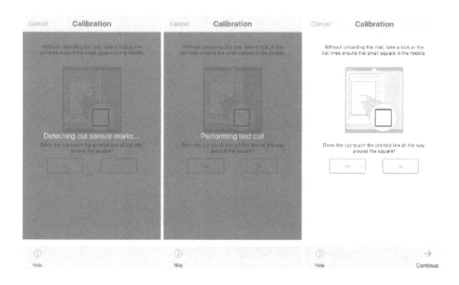

Note: If you choose No, the Design Space will go to the next step to get closer to the line.

7. Your Cricut Explore Air 2 will start the calibration cut on the page's top and side. Once it is done, using Without Unloading the mat, check the line along the page's top and side closely. It is possible for some not to touch the printed lines. Design Space will ask you to choose the numbers and letters cuts that are very close to the printed lines' center. Choose the Top then right-click to give a dropdown that shows the line number or letter with cuts that are very close to the line's center. Once done, choose Continue.

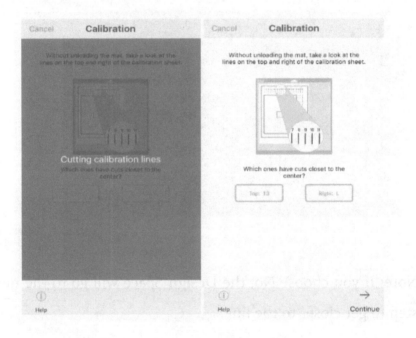

8. Your machine will now perform a confirmation cut just around the large rectangle on the sheet. When done, unload the mat, take the calibration sheet away, and answer the Design Space's final question.

If you are satisfied with the cut, choose Done to save the settings and return to the Home screen.

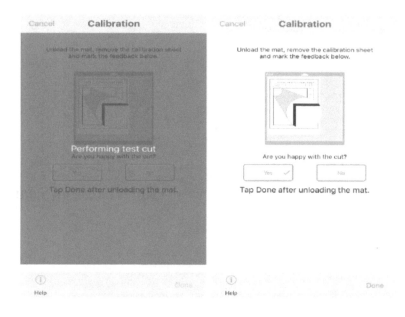

If you are not satisfied and choose No, the screen will guide you in the calibration steps to resolve the issues.

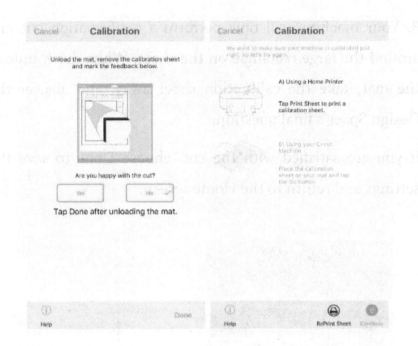

9. Now Print Then Cut.

If you still require some help with Print Then Cut, contact the Member Care

**Chapter 4**

# CRICUT EXPLORE AIR 2 DESIGN SPACES

This chapter is about how to master your Design Space with tips and tricks.

## SYSTEM REQUIREMENTS FOR DESIGN SPACE

As discussed in other chapter Design Space is a free App for Cricut machines that is available for Mac, Windows, Android, and iOS. The current system requirements are listed below:

Note that the requirements presented below may at any time.

**For Windows OS**

Windows 7 is no longer supported. You have to upgrade to the recent version of Windows.

**Operating System:** Windows 8 or recent

**Central Processing Unit:** Intel Dual-Core or AMD processor (equivalent)

**RAM:** 4GB

**Display:** 1024px x 768px (Minimum) screen resolution.

• It must have 2 GB free disk space.

• Bluetooth enabled or Free USB port connection.

**Internet**

• It must be a Broadband connection.

• Min 2 to 3 Mbps Download.

• Min 1 to 2 Mbps Upload.

**Offline**

• Offline is available for Design Space for iOS and Desktop devices only.

• Memory needed to vary based on the projects.

**For Mac OS**

macOS 10.12 or lower versions are no longer supported.

**Operating System:** macOS 10.13 or later.

**Central Processing Unit:** 1.83 GHz.

**Display:** 1024px x 768px (Minimum) screen resolution.

**RAM:** 4GB.

• It must have 2 GB free disk space.

• Bluetooth enabled or Free USB port connection.

**Internet**

• It must be a Broadband connection.

• Min 2 to 3 Mbps Download.

• Min 1 to 2 Mbps Upload.

**Offline**

• Offline is available for Design Space for iOS and Desktop devices only.

• Memory needed to vary based on the projects.

**For iOS Devices**

Below devices are supported:

iOS 12 or later

iPhone

iPhone X, 8, 8 Plus

iPhone 7, 7 Plus

iPhone SE

iPhone 6s, 6s Plus, 6, 6 Plus

iPhone 5s

iPad

iPad Pro 12.9-inch

iPad Pro 10.5-inch

iPad Pro 9.7-inch

iPad Pro 12.9-inch

iPad Air 2, mini 4, mini 3, Air, mini 2

iPod

iPod touch

## Internet

• It must be a Broadband connection.

• Min 2 to 3 Mbps Download.

• Min 1 to 2 Mbps Upload.

**Offline**

• Offline is available for Design Space for iOS and Desktop devices only.

• Memory needed to vary based on the projects.

**For Android Devices**

**Below devices are supported:**

• Android 6.0 or higher.

• Mobile devices and tablets only.

• Chromebooks not supported.

**Supported devices**

**Samsung:** Galaxy S, Galaxy Note, Galaxy Tab A, Galaxy Tab S Series

**Google:** Pixel series

**LG:** G, K, or V series

**Motorola:** Droid G, Z, E, Turbo or Moto series

Note that the performance of each device will depend on the manufacturer, chipset, and processor speed.

**Internet**

• It must be a Broadband connection.

• Min 2 to 3 Mbps Download.

• Min 1 to 2 Mbps Upload.

**Offline**

• Offline is available for Design Space for iOS and Desktop devices only.

• Memory needed to vary based on the projects.

• Remember that Design Space is not compatible with Unix/Linux or Chromebooks computers.

# DESIGN SPACE OPTIONS COMPARISON

Table below shows an easy to ready comparison of cricut Design Space options that are available across Design Space platforms.

| Options | Windows/Mac | iOS App | Android App |
|---|---|---|---|
| Attach | Yes | Yes | Yes |
| Bluetooth compatible | Yes | Yes | Yes |
| Contour | Yes | Yes | Yes |
| Cut and write in one step | Yes | Yes | Yes |
| Flatten to print | Yes | Yes | Yes |
| Writing style fonts | Yes | Yes | Yes |
| machine setup | Yes | Yes | Yes |
| Print then cut | Yes | Yes | No |
| Slice & Weld | Yes | Yes | Yes |
| System fonts | Yes | Yes | Yes |

| | | | |
|---|---|---|---|
| Offline | Yes | Yes | No |
| Photo Canvas | No | Yes | No |
| 3D layer visualization | No | Yes | No |
| Smart Guides | No | Yes | Yes |
| SnapMat | No | Yes | No |
| Pattern fills | Yes | No | No |
| Template | Yes | No | No |
| Image upload | Yes | Yes | Yes |
| Link Physical Cartridges | Yes | No | No |
| Curve Text | Yes | No | No |
| Knife Blade cutting | Yes | No | No |

# DESIGN SPACE FOR DESKTOP
# INSTALLATION INSTRUCTIONS

To be able to install the Design Space on your Desktop.

Prerequisites:

Internet connection

**Windows**

**Steps:**

1. Launch your browser and click on https://design-beta2.cricut.com/#/download.

2. Choose Download.

3. Choose the downloaded file in your preferred folder and Open or Run it.

4. Depending on the computer settings; it may ask if you trust the application. Select the option that you believe the application.

5. There will display installation progress on the screen.

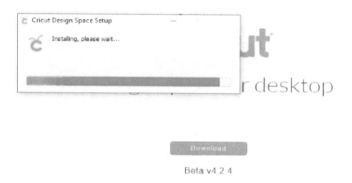

Beta v4 2 4

6. Sign in if you not a new user or Create a Cricut ID if you are a new user.

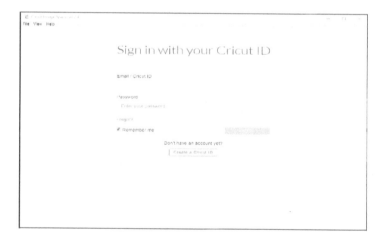

7. The Design Space will be automatically added to your screen. Right-click the icon and pick Pin to the taskbar or you drag the icon to the taskbar to be able to have a shortcut for easy access.

**8.** It is time to start using your Design Space.

**Mac**

**Steps:**

1. Launch your browser and click on https://design-beta2.cricut.com/#/download.

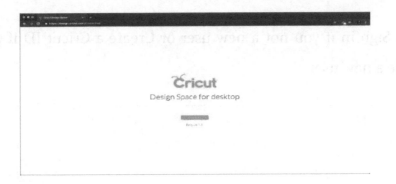

2. Choose Download.

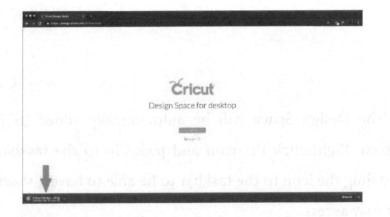

3. Choose the downloaded file in your preferred folder and Open or Run it.

4. Open the installer on the screen.

5. Move the Cricut icon to the Application folder to start the installation. The Design Space will be added to the application folder.

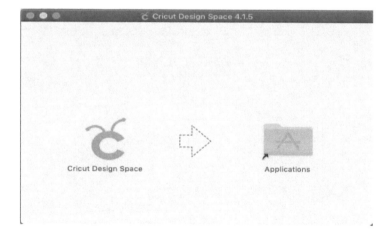

6. Choose Cricut Design Space in the Application folder to open the Design Space from the Desktop application. You may drag the application to the dock to pin it for easy access.

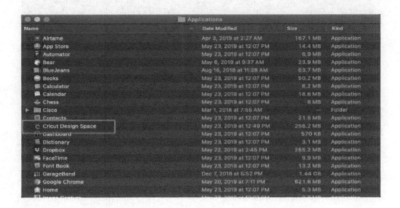

7. A notice may pop to ask if you want to open it, choose Open to continue.

8. Sign in if you not a new user or Create a Cricut ID if you are a new user.

9. It is time to start using your Design Space.

# HOW TO LAUNCH DESIGN SPACE ON DESKTOP

Launching design Space on the Desktop is straightforward. Simply follow the following steps.

**Windows**

**Steps:**

1. Choose the Windows icon or look for the Search box on your screen.

2. Input Design Space into it.

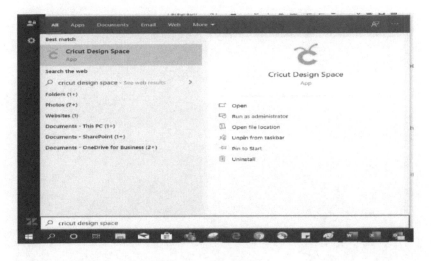

3. Choose the Cricut Design Space that comes up and open the app.

Note: To pin the shortcut to your Desktop environment, simply choose Pint to Start or Pin to Taskbar.

**Mac**

**Steps:**

1. Click the Finder, and choose Applications.

2. Look for the Cricut Design Space app on your system.

3. Double-click to open the app.

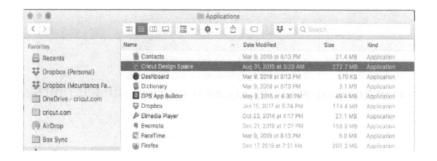

# HOW TO SELECT MACHINE ON DESIGN SPACE

There is a dropdown menu on the Design Space to select the Cricut machine model.

**Windows**

**Steps:**

1. Sign in to Design Space with your Cricut ID and your password.

2. At the upper right corner, there is a dropdown menu to select the model of the Cricut machine you want to use.

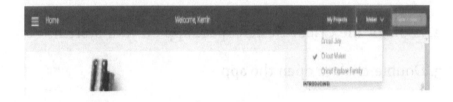

3. The dropdown will display all the Cricut models on Design Space.

# iOS

## Steps:

1. Navigate to the Design Space app for iOS and sign into your Cricut ID and your password.

2. Open the Design Space menu and choose machine Selection.

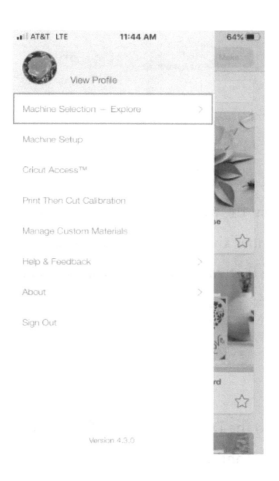

3. Pick the model you want to use

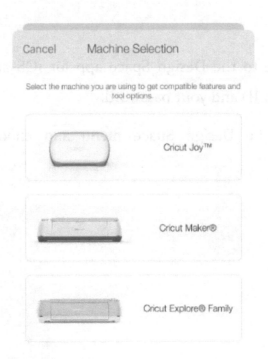

Cancel     Machine Selection

Select the machine you are using to get compatible features and
tool options.

Cricut Joy™

Cricut Maker®

Cricut Explore® Family

4. Select from the available Linetype, Material selection, and tool. Remember that only options that are compatible with the Machine that you want to use will be available.

**Android**

**Steps:**

1. Navigate to the Design Space app for Android and sign into your Cricut ID and your password.

2. Open the Design Space menu and choose machine Selection.

3. Pick the model you want to use.

4. Select from the available Linetype, Material selection, and tool. Remember that only options that are compatible with the Machine that you want to use will be available.

# FUNCTIONS OF DESIGN SPACE

After you have downloaded and installed the Design Space software, the next is to know how to navigate it and use all the software tools to turn your imaginations into realities.

## Canvas Overview

This is a platform where your projects are created. You have to learn about all the tools and icons that are on Canvas.

## Machine selection

You use this to select the type of Cricut machine you want to use. This will let you access features and tools that are only for that specific machine.

## Edit Bar

With this feature, you will be able to access options like color Palette, Linetype, Align, and more to help edit text and images.

## Layer panel

This feature will help you know how to work with design layers like contour, Slice, Group/Ungroup, Attach, and Weld.

### Color Sync Panel

Use this option to drag your colors and drop them to match layer colors of your choice.

### Selecting Linetype

This option communicates with your machine about the way to work with the materials you supply. With this feature, you will be able to tell your Cricut machine how to Cut or Draw.

### Curving Text

Use Curving text to curve so to bend the text box on the Canvas to make a circular shape.

### Using Fonts

On Canvas, personalize your works with different kinds of fonts. You must know how to select fonts, add text, and others.

### Using Images

You must learn how to search, insert, and filter images in your Canvas.

### Using Ready-to-Make Projects

On your Canvas, you must be able to search, filter, and be able to use ready-to-use arts.

**Slice Tool**

Use this feature to cut a shape out of an image or to cut to size with Slice.

**Weld Tool**

With this tool, you will be able to join a letter or customize shapes and cut to be a single piece.

**Attach Tool**

Use the Attach tool to hold the draw layers so to cut layers and lock design placement.

**Contour Tool**

Use this to hide cuts paths that are not necessary for an image.

# CANVAS OVERVIEW ON DESIGN SPACE

The Design Space canvas is where you will be able to design your projects. On the Canvas, project, texts, and images can be edited.

Prerequisite:

Apply only to Design Space on Windows and Mac Computers.

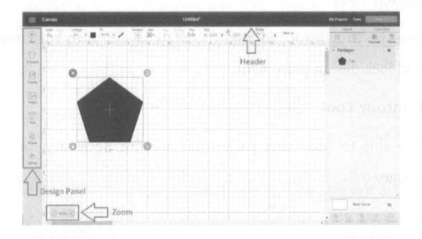

## Design Panel

New: Tap this icon to start a new project.

Templates: Make use of the template to visualizing the finished Project.

Projects: Search, pick and cut projects from the Project Tab.

Images: search, pick, and insert images from the Cricut image library. Also, from the images you uploaded to the canvas.

Text: Use this to write words and sentences unto the Canvas.

Shapes: With this tool, you can add shapes such as squares, circles, and triangles, to the canvas.

Upload: Cut your preferred material and upload in any of these formats, .jpg, .png, .gif, .svg, or .bmp image for free.

**Header**

Menu: Go through the Design Space. With this tool, you can navigate to Canvas, Home, and other features like New Machine, Settings, Link Cartridge, Setup, help, and Sign Out.

Page Title: This tool will remind you where you are on Design Space, is it Home or Canvas? Clicking on Page Title will close an open tab.

Project Name: This is where you will put the name of your Project if it has not been saved.

My projects: Use this tool to open previously saved projects.

Save: With this tool, you can save your projects to your account, for it to be accessible on iOS, Android, Windows, and Mac. Click on Save As to rename the Project.

Make it: Use this tool to prepare the mats and send to the Project on your Machine.

**Zoom:**

Zoom In: To get closer at the Project.

Zoom Out: To have a better view of the Project.

# HOW TO SAVE FOR OFFLINE USE ON DESIGN SPACE FOR DESKTOP

The following steps will help you in saving projects, fonts, and images for use while offline.

**Projects**

**Steps:**

1. Go to the My Projects page and click the three dots on the project tile to be saved. Then pick Save for Offline.

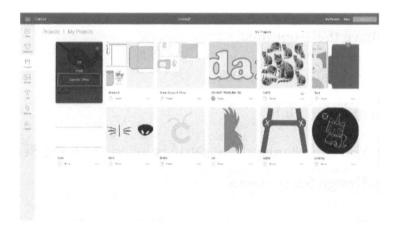

2. There will display a small computer icon on the project tiles you have saved successfully for offline use.

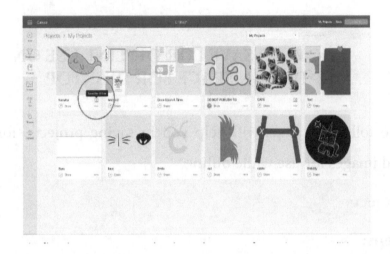

3. You will be directed to a save settings dialogue to pick where to save the projects if there is the first time you are saving a project.

 You have these options:

• Save to Cloud & Computer

• Save to Cloud Only

Note: You can change these settings by going to the Settings in the Design Space menu.

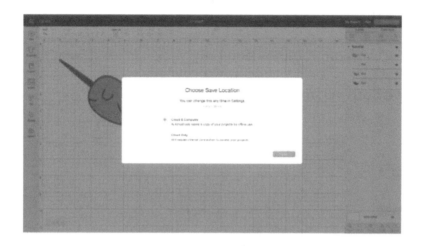

4. Whenever you open a saved project, and there seems to be a conflict between a saved project while offline and a save project in the cloud, a dialogue will pop up that will ask you to choose which version you want to keep.

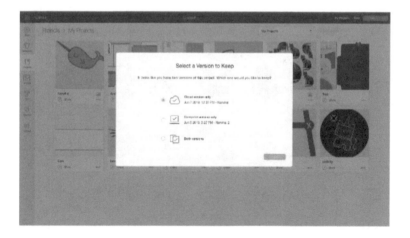

You have these options:

• Save the Cloud version only

• Save the Computer version only

• Save Both versions

**Images**

**Steps:**

1. Navigate to the images tab on the canvas if you want to save images for offline.

2. From here search and Filter for your preferred images. Download the images for offline use by picking the images and choose the Download button in the bottom left corner.

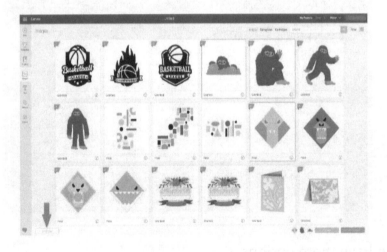

3. The selected images will download once, and after the Computer, an icon will display the image tile to confirm that they have been downloaded successfully.

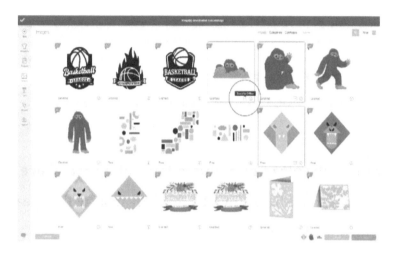

**Fonts**

The fonts on your Computer are installed that you don't need to download them for offline use again.

**Steps:**

1. Go to the fonts menu on the canvas and save Cricut fonts.

2. Here download any font by placing your mouse over the font and choosing the Download button that appears on the right side of the font.

3. Start the download of multiple fonts at a time. Once they have been successfully downloaded, an icon will appear on the right side of the font.

# HOW TO USE DEEP LINKING ON DESIGN SPACE FOR DESKTOP

Deep linking is a way by which Design Space links that are shared through social media, sites, and email will be redirected automatically to Design Space for Desktop.

**Steps:**

1. Click the Design Space links sent to you, and you will be directed to a page. This page will allow you to open the link in the desktop application, or you can download the application (Mac).

2. If you have not installed the Design Space for Desktop, you will be directed to download and open the link.

3. If you have installed Design Space and signed in, select the Open button and it will open the link in the desktop app.

4. But if you have installed but not sign in to the app, you will be taken to sign in before it will open the link.

5. If you have not download and install the desktop app, immediately you click Open, it will take you to a page that asks you to download the app.

6. Once it has been downloaded and installed confirm to re-link the link to be opened in the desktop app so to get to the Project in the Design Space for Desktop.

# HOW TO SELECT LINETYPE ON DESIGN SPACE

Work such as Engrave, Cut, Wavy, Perf, Draw, Deboss, and Score is known as Linetype. Linetype will tell Cricut machine how to handle a project.

**Windows/Mac**

**Step:**

1. Click the dropdown menu to select the Machine you want to use. This option only makes the Linetype options to be worked on be for the Machine earlier picked from the dropdown menu.

2. Insert the preferred images or texts to the canvas.

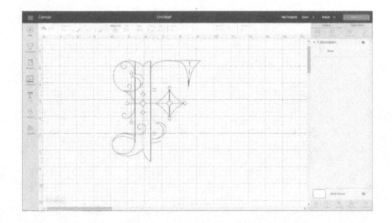

3. Select the Edit bar from the Linetype dropdown. The Linetype shown is will be selected, and other options available to that device will be displayed.

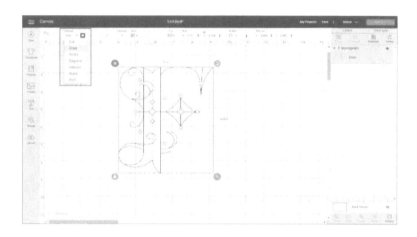

4. Pick your desired Linetype. Once it has been picked the image on the Canvas will change to your selection, and the Linetype will be on the Layers panel.

## iOS

**Steps:**

1. Select Machine Selection from the main menu, then choose your Machine. This option only makes the Linetype options to be worked on be for the Machine earlier picked from the dropdown menu.

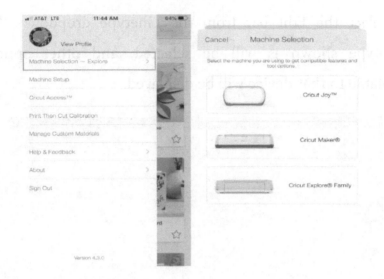

2. Insert the preferred images or texts to the canvas.

3. Select the Edit tool from the bottom of your screen. The display Linetype is pre-selected, and other options available to that Machine will be displayed.

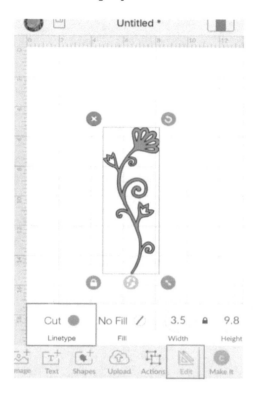

4. 4. Pick your desired Linetype and then tap Apply at upper right corner.

5. The image on the Canvas will change to your selection, and the Linetype will be on the Layers panel.

**Android**

**Steps:**

1. Select Machine Selection from the main menu, then choose your Machine. This option only makes the Linetype options to be worked on be for the Machine earlier picked from the dropdown menu.

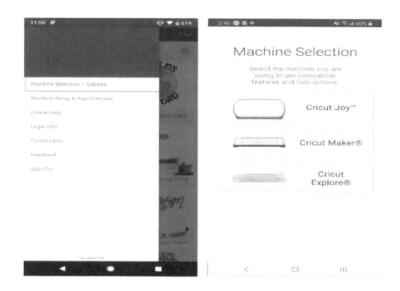

2. Insert the preferred images or texts to the canvas.

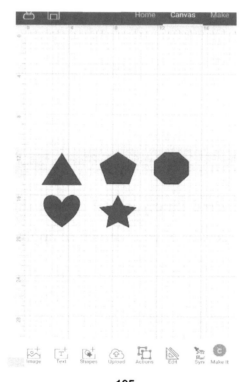

3. Select the Edit tool from the bottom of your screen. The display Linetype is pre-selected, and other options available to that Machine will be displayed.

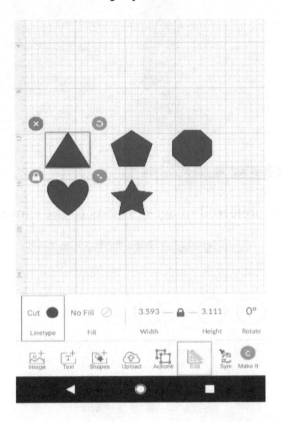

4. Pick the preferred Linetype and choose the checkmark in the upper right corner of your screen to apply.

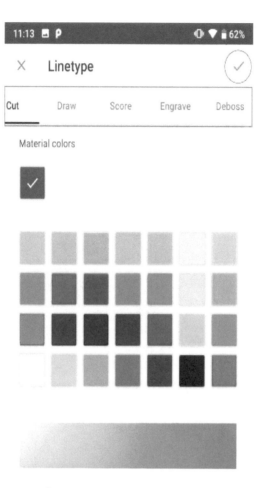

5. The image on the Canvas will change to your selection, and the Linetype will be on the Layers panel.

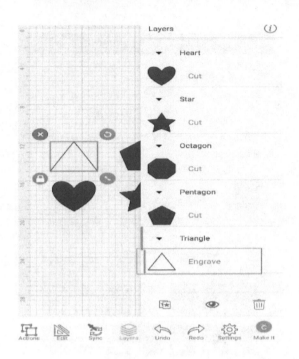

108

# HOW TO USE IMAGES IN DESIGN SPACE

There are over 100,000 images in the Cricut Image Library, and more are being added all the time. Design Space affords the opportunity to use ant image for design before you buy it. So to be sure if it will work well with your Project. You also have the chance to upload your images and cut them with Cricut machine.

**Steps:**

1. Sign in to your Design Space and create a new project.

2. Select Images on the left corner on Windows/Mac computers. Or select the image button at the bottom of your mobile device on Android/iOS.

3. Browse, look and filter images preferred.

All Images: see features images, or you can search for a particular image from the Cricut library.

Categories: Look for images by picking one of the image categories.

Cartridges; Browse an alphabetically the list of 400+ Cricut cartridges (image sets).

4. You may choose multiple images and place them in your Project at the same time.

5. Once inserted you can edit them as you want.

Top right: Use this to rotate the image

Top left: use this to delete the image

Bottom right: use this to size the image

Bottom left: Use this to unlock/lock the image properties

Other features are;

Image Tile: To be able to preview the image

Information: Select the information button to view the name of the image.

Enhanced Printable Images: These give out the images that are already designed with patterns and can be printed and cut.

# HOW TO USE FONTS IN DESIGN SPACE

With Design Space, you can personalize your Project with text and various fonts. You have the liberty of using Cricut fonts and any other system font installed on computers or mobile devices.

**How to add text**

**Steps:**

1. Select text tool from the panel to insert text at the left side of the Canvas. Select text at the bottom of the mobile screens (iOS/Android).

For Windows: Text Edit bar and a text box will be displayed.

For iOS/android: Font list will be opened.

2. Pick your preferred font. Then type your text in the text box.

3. Choose an area outside the box to close it. After this, you can rotate, move, and size the text.

4. To edit text: Double-click the text, and the text box will open. Options to adjust the fonts can be accessed through Edit bar.

**Windows/Mac:**

**iOS App:**

**Android App:**

## How to select a font

Text Editor Tool in the Cricut Design Space works just like Image Edit tool when rotating, sizing, and positioning the texts. This tool also makes it easier to get the right font and be able to edit them to personalize.

Once you select your text, a bounding box will appear. There are options around the box that will help you in editing the text.

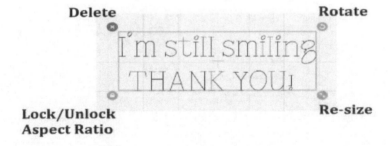

# HOW TO USE SYSTEM FONTS

System fonts are fonts installed on the computer or mobile devices. Design Space is created to automatically access the system font each time there is a need for it free, and you sign in to your Design Space.

**Windows/Mac**

**Steps:**

1. Choose Text from the design panel at the left canvas.

2. The Text Edit bar will display, and you have the liberty to choose a font first or text.

3. Tap on the Font dropdown menu. Choose the System and the font list will be refreshed and show only the installed fonts on the devices.

4. Pick your preferred font and begin to type your text on the screen.

# HOW TO USE TEMPLATES IN DESIGN SPACE

This is just a way to use a template to visualize your desired dreams.

Note: templates are not available in the Design Space App of Mobile devices (iOS/Android) and Cricut Basic App presently.

**Steps:**

1. Choose templates tool in the Design Space at the left side of the Canvas.

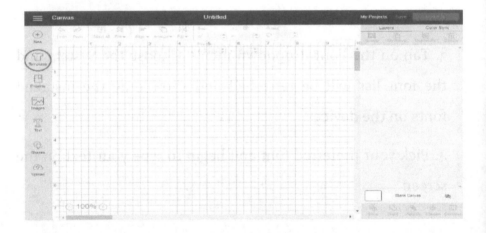

2. Navigate through the various templates and choose a category to peruse the templates. Or make use of the search

field for a specific type of template.

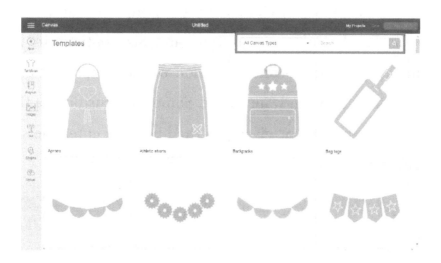

3. Once you pick a template, it will be added to your canvas screen. You will receive alert that the templates are for reference only and is not your Project.

4. Your canvas screen will automatically Zoom out for the whole template to be viewed and the template Edit bar will be displayed. Make use of Type and Size options in the template Edit bar to pick a version of the template that is near to the item you want to use. Some have customs option in the Size panel that gives you the liberty to enter the size manually.

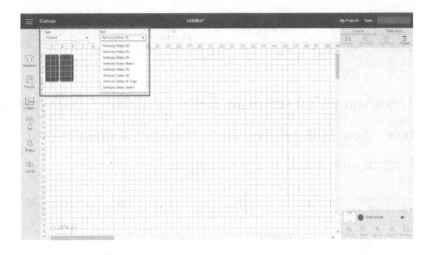

5. Choose template color swatch at the bottom of the Layers panel to change the color of the template.

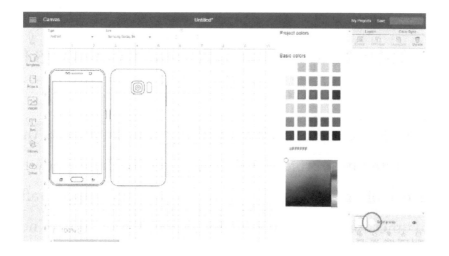

6. Pick the template at the bottom of the Layers panel to dismiss the template. You can now delete the icon at the top.

# HOW TO USE READY-TO-MAKE PROJECTS IN DESIGN SPACE

Design Space comes with some Ready-to-make projects that are created by a professional artist. Some of these ready-to-make projects include home decors, fashion, paper crafts, and other various projects. No forgetting introduction of new projects on a regular basis.

To access these features, simply go to the Design Space page and scroll through hundreds of ready-to-Make projects.

**Steps:**

1. Use the category menu or search bar to select a project category at the top of your screen (Windows/Mac computers), or look at the top of your mobile devices (iOS/Android) in the Design Space App.

**Design Space - Windows/Mac**

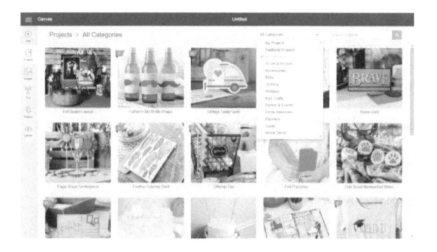

## Design Space - Mobile App

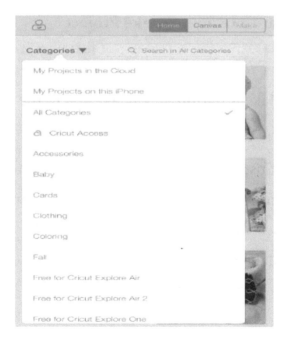

2. Click the Project you prefer. The details of such Project will be opened, such as;

• Project name.

• Estimated Completion Time.

• Difficulty level.

• Cost of the Project.

• Instructions.

• Materials required.

**How to create a ready-to-make Project**

**Steps:**

1. Click on Make It button. It will take you to the mat preview screen.

2. Click on Customize button. It will take you to the design screen. From here you can adjust or add new images to the file, then click Save to keep the Project in your account and then press Make It.

## Design Space - Windows/Mac

## Design Space - Mobile App

# HOW TO UPLOAD IMAGES INTO DESIGN SPACE

With Design Space, you can upload your images for free and make them be converted into cuttable shapes. Basic and vector are two different types of images that can be uploaded.

Basic Images: These images are also known to be called raster images; they include .bmp, .jpg, .png, and .gif files. All these types of files are single layer and can be edited during the uploading process.

Vector Images: Vector images include .dxf and .svg file types. They will upload has been previously designed and be separated automatically into layers after been uploaded.

Note: DXF files are not compatible with Design Space for Android and iOS presently.

**Windows/Mac**

**Steps:**

1. Choose Upload Image on the design panel at the left side of the Canvas. A window will open that will ask you to select an image or pattern to upload. The feature Upload Image will allow you to work with basic image types, that include .png, .jpg, .bmp, and .gif image files and also vector images, that include .dxf and .svg files.

2. Choose Browse and open the file selector and find where the image is located in your Computer, or you just drag and drop the file into the upload window. If you choose .png, .jpg, .bmp, or .gif file to upload you will be directed through the Basic image upload process, and if it is the vector image you will be directed through the Vector image upload process.

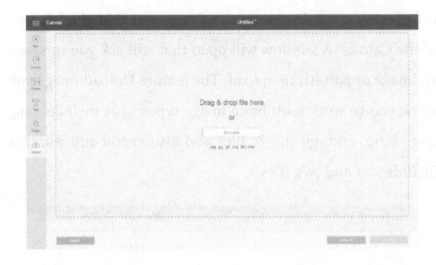

## How to Upload Basic Image

## Steps:

1. Choose the .png, .jpg, .bmp, or .gif file to be uploaded, then pick Open in the file or it can be dragged and dropped into the Design Space window.

2. Decide if the image is moderately complex, simple, or complicated based on its descriptions. Then select Continue.

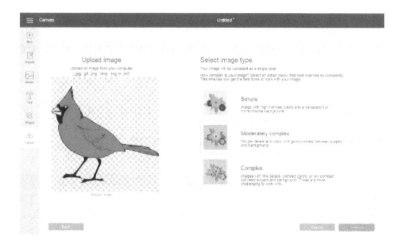

3. Make use of Select & Erase Crop tools, and erase here to get rid of not useful background from the image. Remember that checkerboard background means that the areas have been removed but will not be cut. While the solid areas indicate, the image can be used on the design screen.

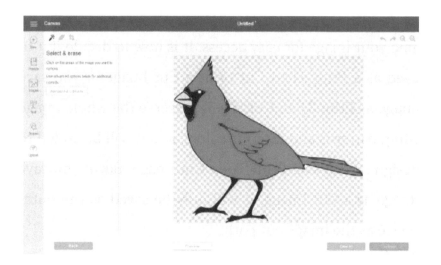

4. Once the unwanted areas have been removed, choose Preview to display the cut lines of the image. If it doesn't display as you want, pick Hide preview to get back to the editing view and readjust the image until you are okay with it. Once you are satisfied, click Continue.

5. Name your image for easy access. It is now to decide if it to be saved as a Print Then Cut or as a Cut Image. If you save the image as Print Then Cut it will preserve the whole image including patterns and interior colors, and it will be added to the design screen as a Print Then Cut image. But if you save the image as a Cut Image, it will only be saved as the outer silhouette as the image cut path.

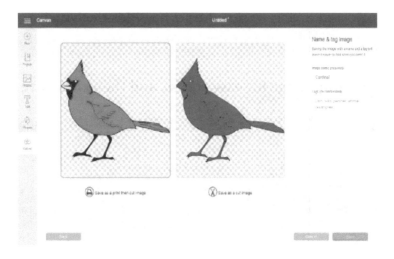

6. Click Save. You will be taken back to the Upload screen, and the new image will be displayed in the uploaded images Library at the bottom of your screen.

7. Tap the image to select and then select Insert Image to be added to your design screen.

**How to upload Vector Image**

**Steps:**

1. Choose .dxf and .svg image you want to upload, then pick Open in the file or it can be dragged and dropped into the Design Space window.

Note: Design Space works with other files designed by other software.

2. Name your image for easy access, and then click Save.

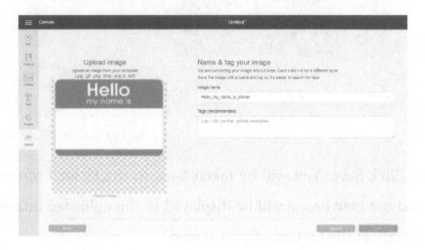

3. You will be taken to upload screen. Your new image will be displayed in the Uploaded Images Library at the bottom of your screen.

4. Tap the image to select and then select Insert Image to be added to your design screen.

5. Your vector images will be displayed on the Canvas as a grouped image. The image layers can be moved and sized separately if ungrouped.

# HOW TO CURVE TEST IN DESIGN SPACE

You can curve your texts with the aid of curve tool in the Design Space to become circular shapes. You can find curve tool in the Text Edit bar located at the bottom of the Canvas in between Advanced tools and Alignment.

Note: Curve tool is presently available for Windows/Mac version of Design Space only.

**Steps:**

1. Tap the text tool in the Design Space located at the left side of the Canvas.

2. Input your text into the text box, select the preferred fonts and style. Make use of the letter Space tool to make the necessary adjustment.

3. Select the Curve tool. Your text will be analyzed for size and space by the Design Space for a few moments, and it will show a slider and a number field.

4. Move the slider to the right to be able to curve the text downward.

Design Space will present a number that is imaginary, and the number determines the curvature of the text.

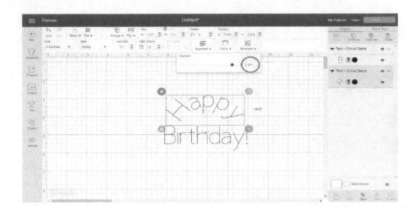

5. Move the slider to the left to be able to curve the text upward. Note the "-" added to the number in the Diameter field.

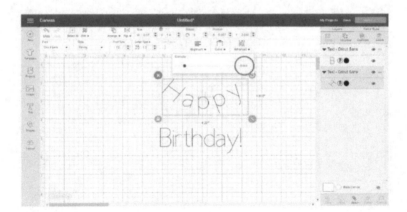

6. If you want to curve multiple texts, match the curvature of the previously curved text quickly by entering the same number manually in the Diameter field.

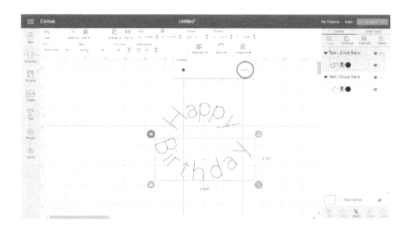

Remember these:

• You can edit Curved text unless flattened or welded. There is still the ability to adjust your curved text in letter spacing, actual text, edit, rotate, font style, and font types.

• Your Curve tool will not work where there are multiple lines of text inside the same text box. The best is to insert different text boxes for each line, or you can use the "Ungroup to Line" tool to drag the lines of text into separate text boxes. Separately curve each.

• Presently projects with curved text will not open in iOS. But if the Project is sliced, welded, isolated or ungrouped for it to act as an image rather than a text box, it will be opened by iOS.

• Project with curved text will open on Android, but you cannot update the curved text. As it will remove the curve.

# HOW TO PRINT THEN CUT IN DESIGN SPACE

How will you like your home printer like inkjet to bring a fantastic project out and you want your Machine to engage the Project in Print Then Cut with high precision without scissor?

Note: This is only for Cricut Explore and Maker.

**How to make your image printable**

To make your image printable, you have to change the Linetype first. To be able to convert multiple layers so to print together, you must make use of Flatten tool located at the Layers panel.

There are Printable images in the library of the Cricut that are pre-designed with decorative patterns. These images show up on the screen ready to Print Then Cut. They will display in the Layers panel has been a single layer and be a Print Linetype. This means that the image can be printed on the home printer, then can be cut on the Cricut Explore or Maker machine.

Click on the Filters icon to find the Printable and check the box marked printable. Choose a Printable, then add to Canvas and pick Make it to Print.

**Windows/Mac:**

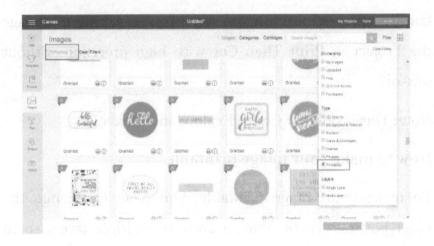

IOS/Android:

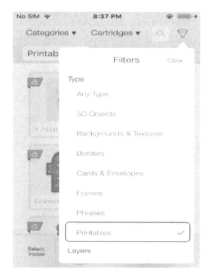

## How to use Print then Cut in projects

**Steps:**

1. As you placed the Printable images or changed the images Linetype to Print, choose Make It from the Design Space. The Preview of the image that was added with cut sensor marking will be displayed. Choose Continue to the cut interaction.

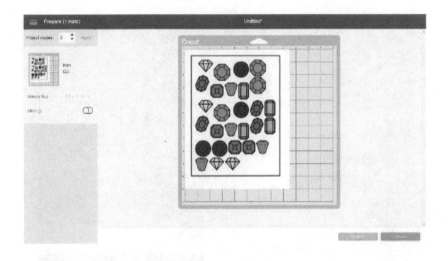

2. Next is to choose your Machine from the dropdown menu. Then pick Send to Printer to open the Print Then Cut box.

3. An image bleed will be applied automatically to the images for it not to have a border when it is cut completely.

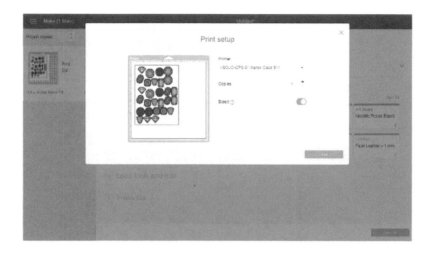

4. Use your home printer to print the page, and then place the paper on the Cricut cutting mat and supply the Cricut machine. It is the duty of the Machine to scan for the sensor marking and then cut around the image with high precision.

Remember these:

9.25" x 6.75" is the maximum image size for Print Then Cut and 8.5" x 11" is the default material size (this info cannot be changed).

Colored, reflective materials or materials that have a pattern that may interfere with the cut sensor mark. So it is better to use Inkjet Printer, and 8.5" x 11" white materials for all Print Then Cut projects (Explore Machine).

...if you have a home printer, print the page and then place

the paper on the flatbed cutting mat and swap the cutting

... time, it is the duty of the machine to scan for the registration marks and then line up the image with the cut precisely.

Reorder-like theme...

...ing is the maximum image size for print lines (14)

and 8.5" ... it is the default material size (print lines cannot be changed)

Colored, reflective materials or materials that have a pattern that may interfere with the cut sensor mark both is harder to the InkjetPrint method of ... some materials for all Print Then Cut projects (Print Machine).

142

# HOW TO FIND FREE IMAGES OF THE WEEK

Cricut in Design Space gives free digital images every week. The followings are the steps that must be taken to find free images for the week.

**Window/Mac**

**Steps:**

1. Sign in to your Design Space.

2. Choose New Project.

3. Choose Image icon from the Canvas on the Design panel.

4. Choose Categories index at the top, and then Free this Week.

**IOS/Android**

**Steps:**

1. Open the Design Space.

2. Start a new project.

3. Press Image from the bottom of the screen.

4. Choose Free this Week under the Categories.

# HOW TO FIND FREE IMAGES, FREE FONTS, AND FREE PATTERNS THAT COMES WITH CRICUT MACHINE

Once the Machine has been completely set up, the free images with Machine will be added to it automatically to your account. The followings are the step to finding your free images on the Machine.

**Windows/Mac**

**Steps:**

1. Sign in to your Design Space.

2. Choose New Project.

3. For free images:

• Tap Images on the design panel of the Canvas.

• Tap the Filter near the search field.

• Tap the Free Filter. This will show all the images that are with your Machine.

4. For Free Fonts:

• Tap Text on the design panel of the Canvas.

• Text Edit bar will show on the screen.

• Tap the Font dropdown menu.

• The Fonts that are free will appear.

5. For Free Patterns:

• Place an image or text.

• Change your file type to Print.

• Choose the color swatch and select Pattern from the Print Type menu.

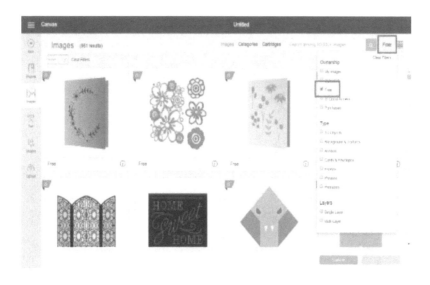

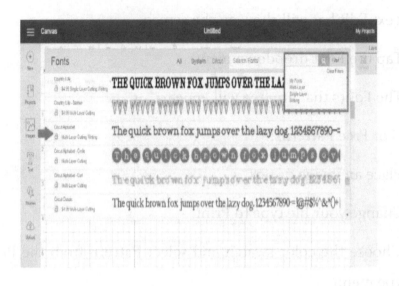

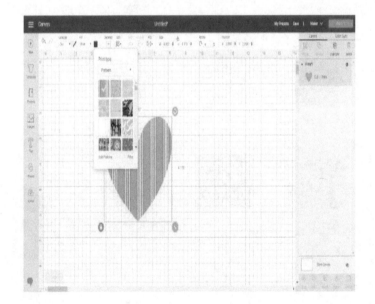

146

**IOS/Android**

**Steps:**

1. Open your Design Space.

2. Choose New Project.

3. For Free Images:

• Press Image from the screen.

• Choose the filter icon.

• Press Free under the Ownership.

4. For Free Fonts:

• Press text from the screen.

• The Font menu will display.

• The Fonts that are free will appear.

• Choose filter icon, and then choose My Fonts under the Ownership to show all fonts that are yours freely.

# HOW TO PURCHASE FROM DESIGN SPACE

You can purchase fonts, images, and ready-to-make projects from the Cricut Library. Follow these steps.

**Windows/Mac**

Open your Design Space menu and make sure you are in the right region. Purchasing items from Design Space is only available presently in the United Kingdom, the United States, and Canada.

You are now to choose what to buy;

1. Images & Fonts.

2. Cartridges (Image sets).

3. Ready-To-make projects.

**How to Purchase Images and Fonts**

**Steps:**

1. Add the images and the fonts you to purchase to your Project first from the dropdown menu.

2. Once you choose Make It, you will be directed to purchase the items that are not free on the Project.

3. Then choose a Purchase button.

4. Review the items to be purchased from the list.

5. Input your payment information with your Cricut password to allow payment.

## How to Purchase cartridges (Image Sets)

**Steps:**

1. Sign in to your Design Space and create a new project.

2. Choose Images in the design panel on the Canvas.

3. Choose Cartridge, then browse or search to finding the item you want to purchase.

4. Choose the Buy button on the cartridge tile or press open the Cartridge, and then pick Buy this Cartridge.

5. Input your payment information on the screen and your Cricut password to allow payment.

## How to Purchase ready-To-Make projects

**Steps:**

1. Sign in to your Design Space and choose View All on any of the project ribbons from the Home page, or Choose Projects in the design panel on the Canvas.

2. Choose a category of ready-to-make projects from the dropdown or search for a specific project.

3. Choose a project to see the details. Tap Make It to go to project preview and buy screen. Choose Customize to launch the Project on the canvas, and then make any necessary adjustment.

4. Choose Make It to go to the project preview, and then choose Purchase.

5. Input your payment information and your Cricut password to allow payment.


**iOS**

On this platform, the purchase is made through Apple iTunes account, and your payment method is saved there.

**How to purchase images and fonts**

**Steps:**

1. Add the images and the fonts you to purchase to your Project first from the dropdown menu in the Edit tool.

2. Once you choose Make It, you will be directed to purchase the items that are not free on the Project.

3. Tap the Purchase button.

4. Review the items to be purchased from the list.

5. Tap Continue.

6. iTunes will process the purchase. Choose Purchase, and then input your Apple ID password and tap Sign In to allow payment.


**How to purchase cartridges (Image Sets)**

**Steps:**

1. Sign in to your Design Space and create a new project.

2. Choose Images on the screen.

3. Choose Cartridge, then browse or search to finding the item you want to purchase.

4. Choose the Buy button on the cartridge tile or press open the Cartridge, and then pick Buy this Cartridge.

5. Review the items to be purchased from the list.

6. Tap Continue.

7. iTunes will process the purchase. Choose Purchase, and then input your Apple ID password and tap Sign In to allow payment.

**How to purchase Ready-To-Make projects**

**Steps:**

1. Sign in to your Design Space. Choose Categories from the Home page. Then from the dropdown select a category of projects.

2. Search or look for the Project you want to purchase.

3. Choose a project to its details. Choose Make It to go directly to the project preview, or you can choose Customize to 'open the Project on the Canvas.

4. Please make the necessary adjustment and choose Make It to proceed to the project preview. Then pick Purchase.

5. Review the items to be purchased from the list.

6. Tap Continue.

7. iTunes will process the purchase. Choose Purchase, and then input your Apple ID password and tap Sign In to allow payment.

**Android**

On this platform, the purchase is made through Google Play account, and your payment method is saved there.

**How to purchase Images and Fonts**

**Steps:**

1. Add the images and the fonts you to purchase to your Project first from the dropdown menu in the Edit tool.

2. Once you choose Make It, you will be directed to purchase the items that are not free on the Project.

3. Tap the Purchase button.

4. Review the items to be purchased from the list.

5. Tap Continue.

6. Google Play will process the purchase in your account, asking you to press Buy. Choose Buy, and input your Google Play password and choose Verify to allow the purchase.

7. Your bought contents are under the Purchase or My Images on the screen.

## How to purchase cartridges (Image Sets)

**Steps:**

1. Sign in to your Design Space and create a new project.

2. Choose Images on the screen.

3. Choose Cartridge, then browse or search to finding the item you want to purchase.

4. Choose the Buy button on the cartridge tile or press open the Cartridge, and then pick Buy this Cartridge.

5. Review the items to be purchased from the list.

6. Tap Continue.

7. Google Play will process the purchase in your account, asking you to press Buy. Choose Buy, and input your Google Play password and choose Verify to allow the purchase.

8. Your bought contents are under the Purchase or My Cartridges on the screen.

## How to purchase Ready-To-Make projects

**Steps:**

1. Sign in to your Design Space. Choose All Categories from the Home page. Then from the dropdown, select a category of projects.

2. Search or look for the Project you want to purchase.

3. Choose a project to its details. Choose Make It to go directly to the project preview, or you can choose Customize to `open the Project on the Canvas.

4. Please make the necessary adjustment and choose Make It to proceed to the project preview. Then pick Purchase.

5. Review the items to be purchased from the list.

6. Tap Continue.

7. Google Play will process the purchase in your account, asking you to press Buy. Choose Buy, and input your Google Play password and choose Verify to allow the purchase.

8. Then click Buy.

# HOW TO PRINT THEN CUT WITH WRITING STYLE FONTS AND IMAGES

With this method, you will be able to change writing style fonts, and images with a line type into Print Then Cut items. You have the option of Print them on a background shape or be printed without background shape and be able to use a punch or cut out by hand.

Remember these:

• 6.75" x 9.25" is the maximum size for Print Then Cut.

• This method is presently not available for Android.

• Compatible with only Cricut Explore and Maker.


**A. Print Then Cut with writing style fonts**

**How to print the writing style fonts on a background shape**

**Steps:**

1. Insert your preferred shape for the Project. Adjust the size and format the shape as you want.

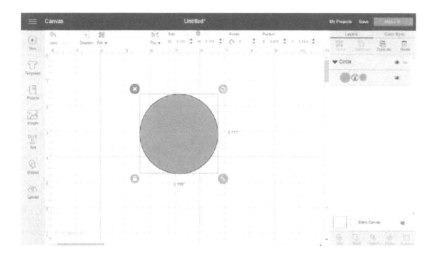

2. Add your text to the Canvas, change to your preferred writing style font, and pick a color for the text. Rearrange the text as you want over the shape. Make sure that the text is entirely within the shape.

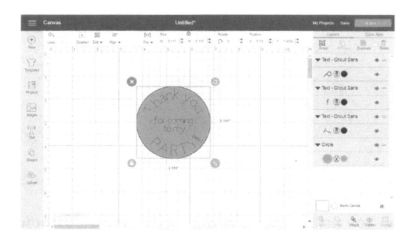

3. Choose All and tap Flatten on the layers panel.

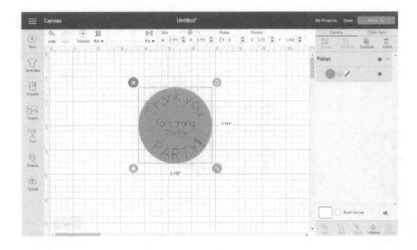

4. Press Make It button to print the image on the home printer and to cut out on the Machine.

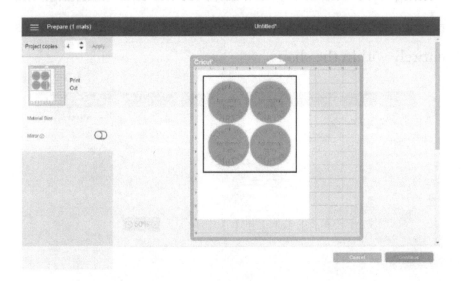

## How to print the writing style fonts without a background shape

**Steps:**

1. Add your texts to the Canvas, Change to a writing style font, and choose the color for the text. Rearrange the text as you want for the Project.

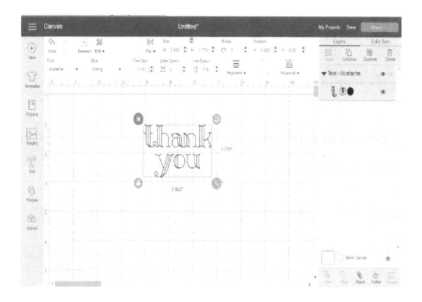

2. Next is to change the line type from Write to Print. Choose the color preferred. Then Press Make It.

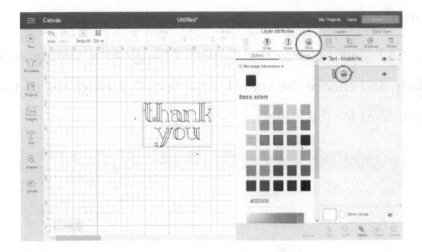

3. Choose and indicate the number of projects copies to be printed, and then press Continue.

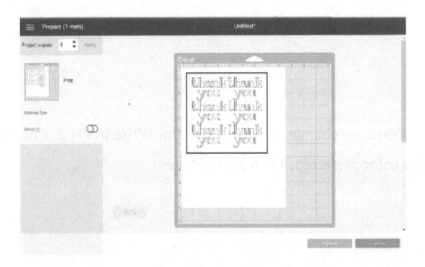

4. Choose Send to Printer, then choose your home printer from the list.

5. Select the number of copies you want.

6. Then click Print.

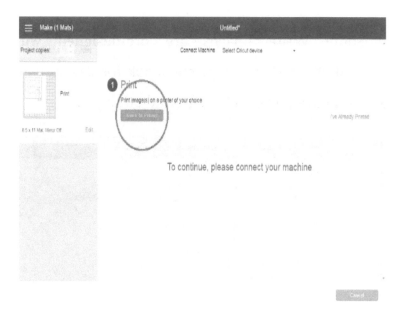

7. Select Cancel to get back to the canvas and it will not load the printed sheets into your cutting machine.

## B. Print Then Cut with writing style images

How to Print Write images on a background shape

With this method, if you want your background shape to print in color, what you will do is to change the color of the shape to white. In as much as the printer does not have a white ink cartridge, it won't print in color.

Steps:

1. Insert your preferred shape into the Project. Do the necessary adjustments on size and format the shape to your taste. Some Write images are pre-designed with a background shape that can be cut. Look for Layers panel to check if you have picked a background cut layer.

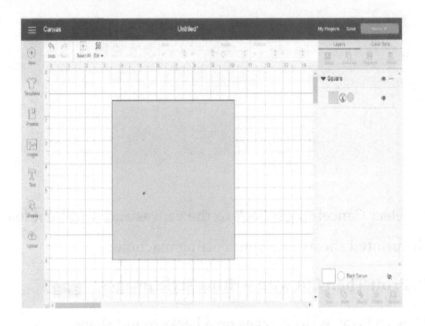

2. Put the Write images to the Canvas. Arrange the image as you want it to be over the shape you pick for the Project and fit within the shape. The image must be kept within the shape.

3. Choose All and select Flatten at the base of the Layers panel.

4. Select Make It button to print the image on the home printer and cut out on the cutting Machine.

**How to Print the write images without a background shape**

**Steps:**

1. Insert a write image to the canvas. If you want to insert multiple Write Images, make use of Attach tool to hold the relative positioning of the images. If the image inserted comes with a background, hide or delete that layer as necessary.

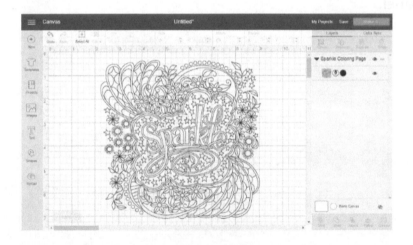

2. Change your line type from the Write to Print. Pick a color you want, then select Make It.

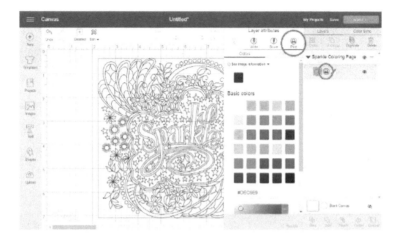

3. Select the number of copies you want.

4. Then click Print.

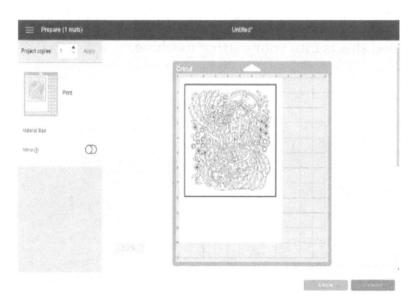

5. Select Send to Printer, choose your home printer from the list and select copies to print.

6. Then click Print.

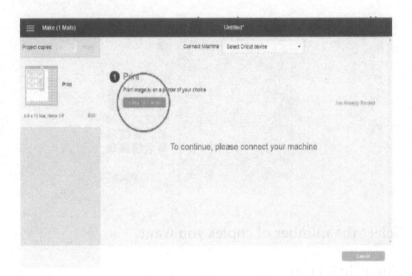

7. Select Cancel to get back to the canvas without loading the printed sheets into your cutting machine.

# HOW TO UPDATE DESIGN SPACE PLUGIN

Design Space for Mac and Windows computers is designed in a way to need plugins. If, as an owner, you receive a notification or you are experiencing some problems with the plugin. It is recommended that you quit the current plugin, and then download and reinstall the plugin again. The following steps are how to go about it.

**Steps:**

1. Stop the current plugin that is giving you issues.

Choose the Design Space plugin from your system file and select Quit or Exit.

Windows                                   Mac

2. Next is to download and reinstall the new Design Space plugin.

Go to https://design.cricut.com, sign in to your Cricut account, and supply your password.

3. Download and reinstall the new plugin.

# HOW TO CLEAR APPLICATION CACHE ON DESIGN SPACE FOR DESKTOP

If you discover that your Desktop is not loading or is bringing out a blank screen, it is caused by application cache. This issue can be resolved by following these steps.

Note: It is recommended to save all your files in the Cloud so as not to be deleted. These steps will delete all the files on your system.

**Windows**

**Steps:**

1. Make sure that the Design Space is closed.

2. Open File Explorer on your system.

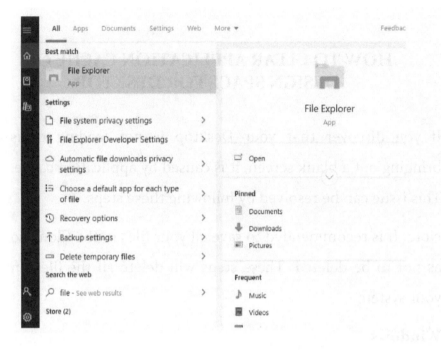

File Explorer
App

3. Choose This PC on your system, and then pick Local Desk (C).

4. Choose Users folder on the system.

5. Open the folder, and you will see a folder named .cricut-design-space.

6. Open the folder, and you will another named LocalData.

7. Open the folder and choose all the folders in the Local Data folder.

8. Press Shift+Delete to delete the files permanently there.

9. The next is to launch your Design Space.

10. Click View on the system menu, and then click Force Reload.

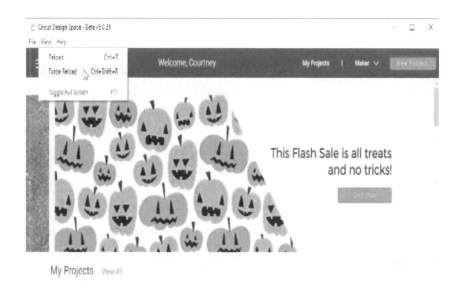

**Mac**

**Steps:**

1. Make sure that the Design Space is closed.

2. Go to the Finder on your system and click Applications.

3. From Applications, click on Terminal.

4. In the Terminal input the following command: defaults write com.apple.finder AppleShowAllFiles YES

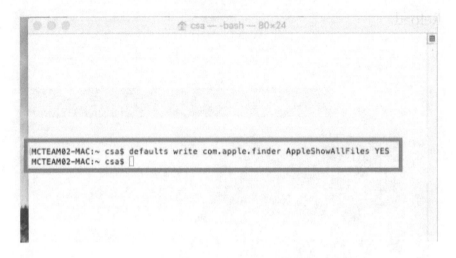

5. Next, id to close the Terminal, and then press Ctrl+click on the Finder.

6. Choose Relaunch on your menu.

7. Choose your hard drive in the Finder.

8. Choose the Users folder.

9. Click on your user account name.

10. Look for a folder named .cricut-design-space and open it.

11. Pick all the files in the LocalDate and drag it to the Trash.

12. Next is to empty your Trash.

13. Finally, launch your Design Space, and then reforce the app, by Choosing View on the system menu and click on Force Reload.

Whenever you want to work on a project, you will need to choose the mat type in Design Space so order the machine if you are going to use Card Mat, Smart Materials, or a machine mat.

## Window/Mac

## Steps:

1. When you are done with the project, and you want to send to the Cricut Explore Air 2, choose Make It. Design Space will

ask if you want to load it with Card Mat, a machine mat, or

Smart Materials.

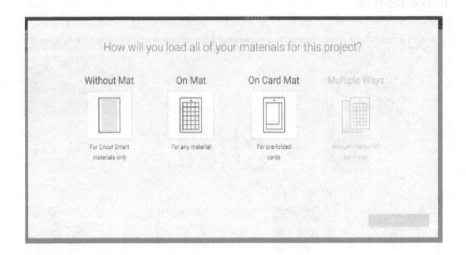

2. Select the option you planned to use for the project. The type of load you choose will determine the material setting options on the screen. An example is Without Mat, it will work for Smart Materials, so it is only Smart Materials will be cut when you choose Without Mat.

3. It is crucial you load the material that matches the type selection. Note that the machine only recognizes the length and not the type of material load. If you choose With Mat, load material that is With Mat.

4. If there is a need for you to change your selection, pick a new type from the dropdown menu on the screen.

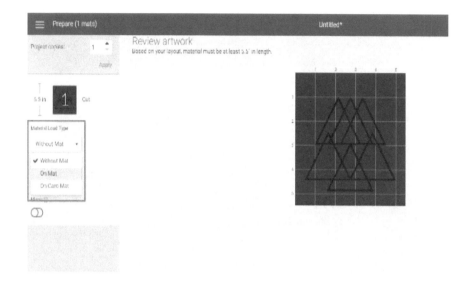

## iOS

## Steps:

1. When you are done with the project, and you want to send to the Cricut Explore Air 2, choose Make It. Design Space will ask if you want to load it with Card Mat, a machine mat, or Smart Materials.

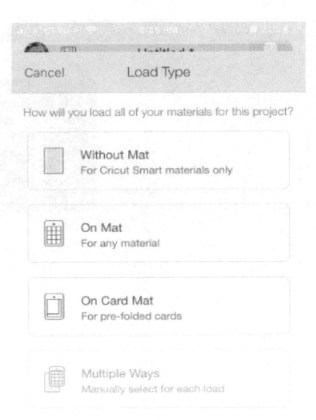

How will you load all of your materials for this project?

Without Mat
For Cricut Smart materials only

On Mat
For any material

On Card Mat
For pre-folded cards

Multiple Ways
Manually select for each load

2. Select the option you planned to use for the project. The type of load you choose will determine the material setting options on the screen. An example is Without Mat, it will work for Smart Materials, so it is only Smart Materials will be cut when you choose Without Mat.

3. It is crucial you load the material that matches the type selection. Note that the machine only recognizes the length and not the type of material load. If you choose With Mat,

load material that is With Mat.

4. If there is a need for you to change your selection, click on the mat settings icon. Then press material Load Type and choose a new Type from the list.

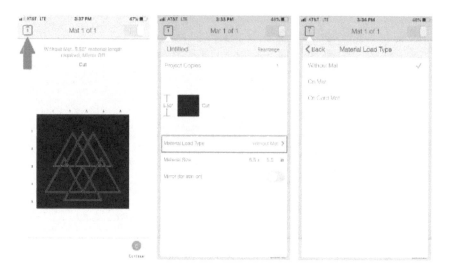

**Android**

**Steps:**

1. When you are done with the project, and you want to send to the Cricut Explore Air 2, choose Make It. Design Space will ask if you want to load it with Card Mat, a machine mat, or Smart Materials.

**Select Material Load Type**

How will you load all of your materials for this project?

**Without Mat**
For Cricut Smart materials only

**On Mat**
For any material

**On Card Mat**
For pre-folded cards

**Multiple Ways**
Manually select for each load

2. Select the option you planned to use for the project. The type of load you choose will determine the material setting options on the screen. An example is Without Mat, it will work for Smart Materials, so it is only Smart Materials will be cut when you choose Without Mat.

3. It is crucial you load the material that matches the type selection. Note that the machine only recognizes the length and not the type of material load. If you choose With Mat, load material that is With Mat.

4. If there is a need for you to change your selection, press the mat setting. Then press select material Load Type and select a new Type from the list.

5. Click Ok to effect the change.

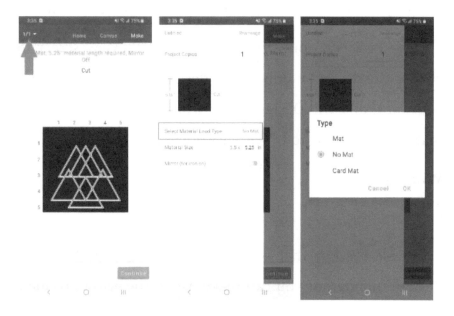

# HOW TO INCREASE PROJECT COPIES

With this method, you can make multiple copies of the same designs, and you can change the number of project copies.

Choose Project Copies from the Project Preview screen to choose the desired number. The design will be duplicated as you want, and the Design Space will add Smart material or mats automatically to the project preview as desired.

**Windows/Mac**

**Steps:**

1. Choose the box that is next to Project Copies. Input the desired number, or you can make use of the arrows to make your number.

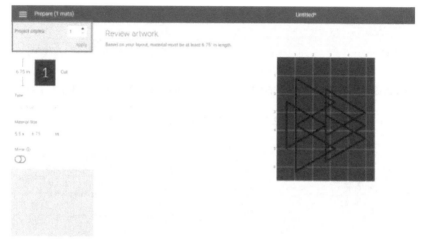

2. Select **Apply**

# 2. Choose Apply.

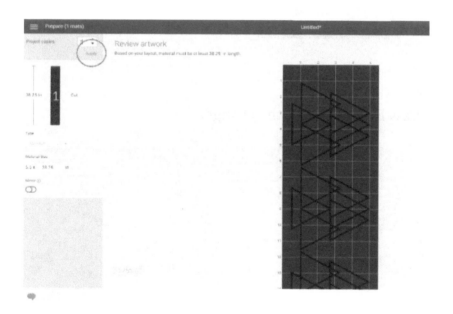

# iOS

## Steps:

1. Press the mat settings icon, and then press the Project Copies field and input your preferred number.

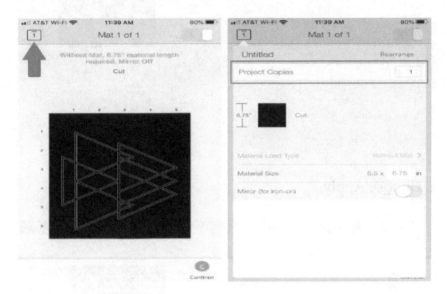

2. Press Done to effect the change.

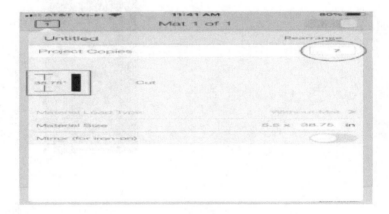

## Android

## Steps:

1. Press the mat settings icon, and then press the Project Copies field and input your preferred number.

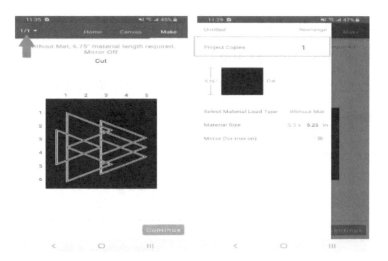

2. Press Done to effect the change.

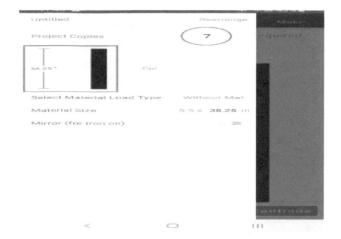

# HOW TO UNDERSTAND THE AMOUNT OF MATERIAL NEEDED

There is a Material Size indicator on the Project Preview screen that will display the amount of material you will need based on your design and the numbers of project copies you input when you want to send the project to the Cricut machine.

Design Space for Desktop

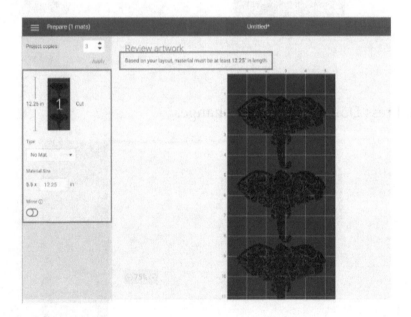

# iOS

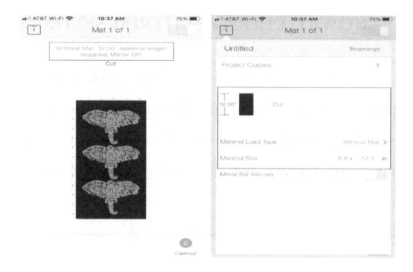

# Android

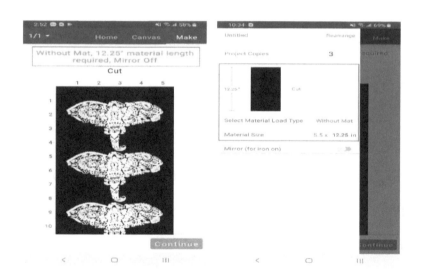

# HOW TO CHOOSE MATERIAL SETTINGS

The moment you connect your Cricut Explore Air 2 to computer or mobile device, material settings will display as a series of tiles on the cut screen. If can see your material among those display, just tap on the tile to choose the setting.

**Windows/mac**

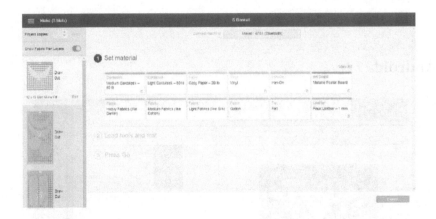

If you don't see your material on the list, simply follow these **steps:**

• Click View All.

• Then click the highlighted places.

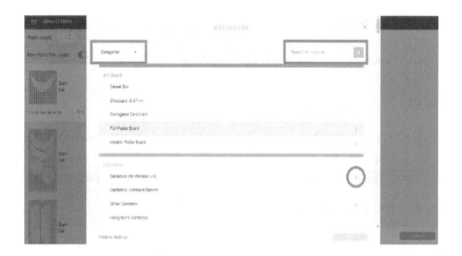

# HOW TO USE OR CREATE OR DELETE CUSTOM MATERIAL SETTINGS IN CRICUT EXPLORE AIR 2

Cricut added some settings that are pre-programmed on Design Space for the buyers to have flexibility while working on various materials for the projects. Buyers of Cricut machines have the ability to choose from these pre-programmed settings, or they decide to create their settings.

**Windows/Mac**

How to use a Custom material setting

**Steps:**

1. Sign in to your Design Space, and open/create a project.

2. Your Cricut machine must have been powered and connected to a computer via Bluetooth.

3. Go to the Project Preview screen.

4. Choose Browse All Materials.

5. Check all the list, making use of the All Categories dropdown, or you may search for the material by name. Note that materials that have Cricut logo beside it are Cricut brand materials.

**How to create a new custom material**

If the material you want to use is not included in the Custom material list, you may check other settings that are very close to the machine settings, or you have the ability to create your own.

Note: It not possible presently to add new Custom material to Android, but anyone added from the Windows/Mac and iOS will be available on the Android platform.

**Steps:**

1. Go to Menu in the Design Space and choose Manage Custom Material or choose Material Setting when you want to pick materials for a project to open the Custom Material screen.

## 2. Move to the base of the list and choose Add New Material

## 3. Be specific about the material and choose Save.

4. Once it is saved, you have the option of;

• Cut Pressure (ability to adjust the slider or making use of +/- buttons).

• Multi-cut (This option ask the machine to cut multiple times on the same image and is the best for thicker materials).

• Blade Type (choose Deep-Point Blade or Fine-Point blade for the Design Space to direct you well).

5. Once you have it configured, then choose Save so to save your new custom material.

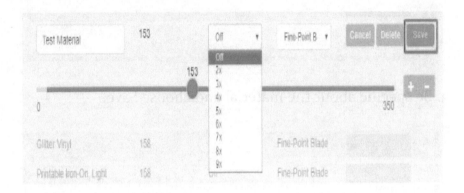

6. Pick the X symbol to close the material screen. The new material is now added to the list of materials, and you can get by using the search box.

## How to Edit or Delete Custom Materials

### Steps:

1. Open the Menu and choose Manage Custom Materials. Move to the Edit button and make the necessary adjustment.

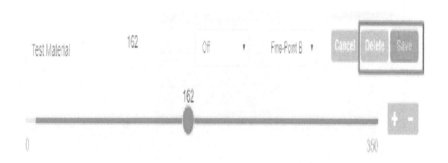

### iOS/Android

## How to use Custom material setting

### Steps:

1. Open the Design Space on your mobile device and open or create a new project.

2. Your Cricut machine must have been powered and connected to your device via Bluetooth.

3. Go to the Project Preview screen.

4. Choose All Materials on the set material screen.

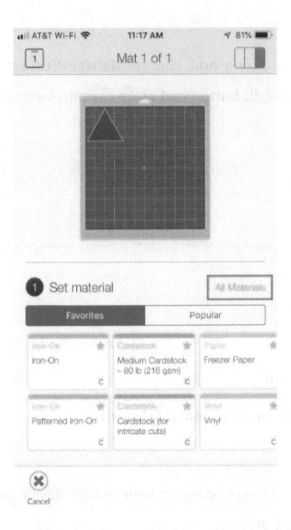

5. Move to check the list, or you can search for a specific material by name. Note that any material that has Cricut logo beside it are Cricut brand materials.

## How to create a new custom material

If the material you want to use is not included in the Custom material list, you may try the closest matching settings, or you have the ability to create your own.

Note: It not possible presently to add new Custom material to Android, but anyone added from the Windows/Mac and iOS will be available on the Android.

**Steps:**

1. Go to Menu in the Design Space and choose Manage Custom Material or choose Material Setting when you want to pick materials for a project to open the Custom Material screen.

2. Choose the + icon on the screen.

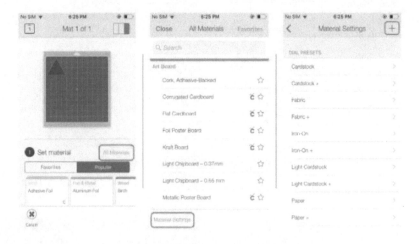

3. Be specific about the material and choose Add.

4. Once it is saved, you have the option of;

• Cut Pressure (ability to adjust the slider or making use of +/- buttons).

• Multi-cut (This option ask the machine to cut multiple

times on the same image and is the best for thicker materials).

• Blade Type (choose Deep-Point Blade or Fine-Point blade for the Design Space to direct you well).

5. Once you have it configured, then choose Save so to save your new custom material.

6. Go to the cut preview screen. Your new material will be available in the list of materials that are available making use of search box.

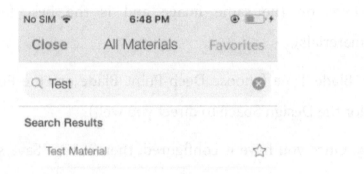

## How to Edit or Delete Custom Materials

**Steps:**

1. Choose the profile icon, then choose Manage Custom Materials.

2. Choose custom material that you want to delete or edit.

3. Make the necessary adjustment and click on Save or Delete.

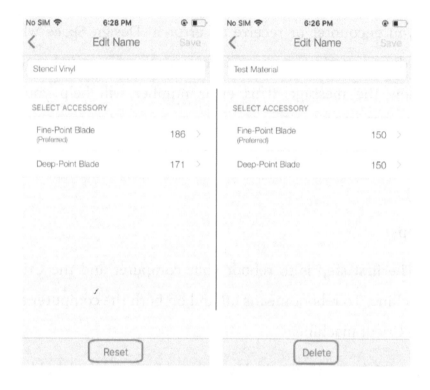

# HOW TO CORRECT DESIGN SPACE NUMBER ERRORS

If you encounter or receive an error in Design Space when sending a project to your Cricut machine, a number will follow the message. This error number will help you in diagnosing the issue encountered. The solution to these error numbers is well discussed below in steps.

**(0)**

**Steps:**

1. The first step is to reboot your computer and the Cricut machine. To reboot means off and on both the computer and the Cricut machine.

Mac: Make sure you do Hard Reset by press and hold the computer power button till the screen goes black and the computer is shut down completely.

2. Check the system requirements of your computer if it meets the specs of the Design Space. If not, get the system that meets the system requirements.

3. The next is to clear the browser history and cookies of your computer. And make sure that it is the supported browser you use.

4. If the error that appears comes with multiple projects and it is for a particular project. It is better to isolate the affected project and recreate it.

5. If all the above steps failed, then try to use another browser on another computer.

6. If all fails, contact Member Care to resolve the issue.

(-2) = **Not Supported**

**Steps:**

1. It is essential to use the Cricut machine that Design Space support. This error will display when you are using the Cricut machine that Design Space is not supporting again.

2. Check if the browser is supported and up to date.

3. Use another supported browser if the issue is not resolved.

4. Check again if the system you are using meets the Design Space requirements. And if not, get another computer that

has the system requirement for the Design Space.

(-3), (-10), (-19)

(-3)= **Device in Use error.**

(-10)= **Device Not Open error.**

(-19)= **Device Already Open error.**

**Steps:**

1. Select the Reset Connection or Retry button to process the machine communication, and attempt to redo your cut again.

2. Make sure that you complete the machine set up. If there are one or two steps that you skip, it will lead to error.

3. After checking if the setup is completed, then look for the color of the machine power button.

Green: Both the Cricut Explore and Maker power button will never change to green. So if their power button is changed to green, know that you are trying to use Design Space with a not compatible machine. It is recommended to use a compatible system with Design Space.

Solid or Steady Red: when the power button is steady/solid red, it is an indication that your machine requires a firmware update. The design Space will detect the firmware version on the device in some moments and ask for updates. Choose the option to update. Meanwhile, if the power button is steady/solid red, and there is no other button that is lit, it indicates a power issue. The solution is to use another power outlet.

Power button Blinking or Flashing Red: It has been discussed previously on how to resolve such issues (check Cricut machine Troubleshooting for details).

Blue: When the power button is displaying Blue, it's an indication that there is a communication between the Cricut machine and Design Space via Bluetooth.

White: White is the standard color for the Cricut Explore power button light. If it's not Cricut Explore, do the followings:

• Connect your device to another USB port on the computer.

• If you are using Bluetooth, disconnect, and reconnect again.

• If all the above suggestions are not working, and then connect your computer through a USB cord. Then try to cut if it fails to move to the next step.

4. Disconnect your machine from the computer and press to off. Once it is entirely off, restarts both the computer and your device. Wait for a few minutes, then launch the Design Space and try to process your project. If it fails, move to the next step.

5. Try to use another supported browser. If it fails, move to the next step.

6. If all the above steps failed to use a different USB cord. Suppose you don't know the standard configuration of the USB, contact the Member Care for assistance.

7. If all the above steps failed, it is advised to contact the member Care for more assistance.

## (-11)= Device Authentication

This is as a result of some programs that are running in the background. It is recommended to close such programs and try your project again.

Make sure that your browser is supported and up to date.

## (-18)= Device Timeout

**Steps:**

1. Off the power of the Cricut Maker/Explore.

2. Terminate the Design Space software.

3. Once it is entirely closed, re-open the Design Space.

4. Power back the Cricut machine and try to cut your project again.

5. If all the above steps fail, get in touch with the Member Care for further assistance.

## (-21)= A data transmission error

**Steps:**

1. Clear the browser history, cache, and cookies from your computer.

2. Terminate, re-open the browser and try to cut the project again.

3. If it fails, use another supported browser to resolve the issue.

4. If it fails, use another network, it may be that you are having an internet dip in speeds.

5. Get to your service provider and make your complaint about assistance.

Another set of the cause of (-21) are;

1. Changes of Scoreline to Print or Cut or was flattened. The solution is to make your design unflattened and remove the Scoreline. Choose and for correct printing flatten the layers, and reattach the Scoreline.

2. Writing style font that was changed to Print or Cut was flattened. The solution is to change the font.

3. Not fully enclosed shape can also cause this error.


(-24)= Ping Timeout error

**Steps:**

1. If you are having issues with multiple projects and the case is only to one of the projects. The problem could be the

project is too large, or you did not save it very well. The solution is to recreate the project and if it fails, go to the next step.

2. Connect the Cricut Maker/Explore machine to your computer with another USB cord port on the computer.

3. Use another different USB cord. The right configuration of USB for Design Space software. Contact Member care for further assistance if you cannot locate the suitable USB cable.

4. Another cause could make the dip in internet speeds. If you have an issue caused by a drop in internet speeds, its either you try another network or contact your service provider to solve the problem.

**(-32)= Firmware Not Available error**

**Steps:**

1. Make sure you are using the right machine (either Maker or Explore or Joy). Attempt to use a device not compatible with the Design Space will bring out this error.

2. If the error continues while using a compatible machine, get in touch with the Member Care for further assistance.

## (-33)= Invalid Material Settings error

**Steps:**

1. To avoid this error, the Smart Set Dial must be set to Custom, and make sure that you choose a material from the Design Space material menu. If the error continues, then go to the next step.

2. Try another material setting to confirm the error. If it fails, contact the Member care for further assistance.

# Chapter 5

# CRICUT EXPLORE AIR 2 TRICKS AND TIPS

## Start with the Sample Project

Once your order of the Cricut Explore Air 2 arrives, begin with the sample project!

The Cricut Explore Air 2 is packaged with sample material for your first project. However, if you purchase a Cricut Everything Bundle, you will receive lots of materials and tools to begin your journey to Cricut cutting. But if you order for Cricut Bundle, it will come with a small number of materials that you will need to start your sample project.

## Make sure your Cutting mat is cover.

Do you realize that your cutting mat comes with a plastic shield? Pull the plastic shield off easily whenever you want to use the mat, and cover it back when you are done using it. This little gesture will keep your mat clean and makes it sticky for a long time.

**Clean the Cutting mat always.**

It is advised to clean your mat most times if you can afford to clean it every time you use it. Cleaning the cutting mat with baby wipes is one of the best ways to clean your cutting mats. Don't forget that the non-alcoholic water wipes without fragrance will work best on your cutting mat. This type of baby wipe will keep the mats from gathering up cardstock and vinyl debris from cutting and other household dust and dirties flying around.

**Subscribe to Cricut Access.**

Though your Design Space comes with some free graphics, font, and images in the Design Space, if you want to get the best out of your Cricut Explore Air 2 machine, it is advised to subscribe to Cricut Access. The Cricut access has three types of plans you can subscribe to. But it is better to start with a monthly plan as it is cheaper, and you have the chance of cancelling the subscription if you are no longer interested.

The Cricut Access is designed in such a way as it will give you unlimited access to over 400 beautiful fonts and 100,000 images. If you are the type that will always want to be using its machine often, Cricut Access will save you lots of money from buying images, fonts, and projects every time.

**Always Set the Dial.**

Don't think that this is the most straightforward rule of the Cricut machine. I can't recollect the number of times I forgot to set the dial. I discovered that it is easy to overlook setting the dial when I have finished creating my designs, and I longed to cut it. The funny thing about this part is that Design Space will ask if the material dial is set when it is about to cut the design.

**Make use of the Right Tools.**

It is crucial to get the right Cricut tools!

The Cricut machine's right set of tools includes tweezers, scrappers, weeding tools, Spatula and Scissors with a protective blade cover.

**Have Cricut Scoring Stylus with you.**

If you always like to create card projects, you have to get a scoring stylus. If you initially don't order a scoring stylus with your bundle, it is advised to request one.

**Always De-tack the Cutting Mat.**

The norm in the operations of the Cricut machine is to place the material to be worked upon on the mat before you put it into the machine. It is expected that when you first buy your machine, remove the plastic that covers the mat, and place a clean, dry cloth over it to make it ready for the first project. This will help your mat in not destroying your project when you are trying to remove it. This issue always happens to the green light grip mat and not to the blue light grip mat.

**Always Test Cuts.**

It is recommended that you always perform a test cut before you start cutting the whole project whenever you are creating your project. This test cut will let know if your blade is set too low as it will ruin the cutting mat, or if the pen is not adequately set to write what you want to see. So performing a test cut checks if your machine has been set right to deliver what you desired.

**Always Replace the Pen lids after use.**

I discovered that I always forget to replace my Cricut pens' lid whenever I have finished a project. To avoid your pens' ink to dry off when you have not used it, always put it in your mind to replace the lids whenever you are done with your projects.

**Another way to remove materials from the cutting mat.**

Apart from the usual way of using the right tools to remove cardstock or vinyl from your cutting mat, there is another proper way to get it off. With this trick, you will be able to peel your work from the mat, just bend the mat away from the card, and your project will be easily removed from the mat.

**Use the right blade for your machine.**

There is nothing that discourages when doing a project than discovered that you are using the wrong tools. For your Cricut Explore Air 2 to cut very well, use the blades recommended in Chapter 1. These blades can be used to cut thicker cards, chipboard, leather, etc. Ensure that when you are to get the blade, you get it with its blade housing.

**Where to get free SVG files**

You may want to have SVG files outside of the Design Space store. With the list of the sites below, you can create your SVG files.

Best Free SVG Sites

https://designbundles.net/free-design-resources/rel=vsLnZD

https://www.creativefabrica.com/freebies/free-crafts/ref/150994/

https://www.3dsvg.com/

https://Craftbundles.com

https://thehungryjpeg.com/

https://sofontsy.com/product-category/free/

https://www.simplycraftysvgs.com/product-category/freebies/

https://www.printablecuttablecreatables.com/product-category/freebies/

https://cutthatdesign.com/

**Load your mat correctly.**

Ensure that the cutting mat is correctly loaded on the machine before you begin to cut. Be sure that the mat is slipped under the machine rollers.

**Circuit's Custom Cut Settings.**

The Cricut Explore Air 2 has the following custom setting:

• Poster band.

• Paper.

• Iron-on.

• Vinyl.

• Bonded fabric.

• Light Cardstock.

• Cardstock.

If you discovered that the material you want to cut is not among the above list, there is an option known as Custom that from there you can choose from the dial.

Simply launch your Design Space, choose your project, and tap Make It. From here, you will be able to select your material from the dropdown list.

**Install Fonts.**

If there is a font you want to use for a project and is not in the Design space. Just download and install the font into your computer. To use this font after downloading and installation, sign out of the Design Space and sign in, and your new font will be displayed in the Design Space. There may not be any reason to restart your computer.

**Replace Your Blades.**

Knows that like every tool and parts, the Cricut blade will indeed wear out. So when you discover that the cuts are no smooth and effective, know that it is time to change it. Other reasons that will make you change the blade are;

• When the vinyl is pulling or lifting odd the backing sheet.

• When the card or vinyl is tearing.

• When the cutting is not through.

• The above reasons indicate that it is time for you to buy a new Cricut blade.

**Use different blades for different materials.**

Please don't use the same blade you are using for cardstock for vinyl. Remember that cardstock is more comfortable to cut for the blade than the vinyl. You have to separate the blade for vinyl and another separate blade for cardstock.

**Mirror Your Images for HTV.**

You need to mirror the design you want to cut for heat transfer, especially with vinyl. After you might have selected the Make It, there is a feature to mirror your design.

# Chapter 6

# CRICUT EXPLORE AIR 2 FIRST DESIGN.

This project sample is just to make you know that you can create a project with the materials that come with your Cricut Explore Air 2.

Launch design.cricut.com on your browser, tap on the menu icon and at the top left corner, and you will see New Machine Set up. Click on it, and you will see a design you will use for your first sample project.

**Materials needed:**

• Cricut Explore Air 2 machine

• Cutting mat

• Cricut Pen

• Cardstock

• Paper

Note: If the protective cover is still on your cutting mat, remove it and set the mat aside.

**Steps:**

1. Place the cardstock on the cutting mat. Ensure that it is the textured side facing up and line the card vertically on the cutting mat. Line the cutting mat up on the top left corner, under your machine logo.

2. Place the cutting mat in the machine. It is advised to press the mat firmly on the rollers while you press the "load/unload" button on the top right corner of the machine.

3. Open the clamp A and place the Cricut pen and close the clamp.

4. Check the design on your screen and preview it again. Then press Go.

5. Set the dial on the Cricut Explore Air 2 to cardstock.

6. Immediately you press Go, the "C" button on your machine will start flashing. Then press the button to start the creation of the design and see the wonder happens.

7. Remove the mat when the project is finished. Press Load/unload button and remove the Cricut pen form the clamp.

8. Place your cutting mat face down on a clean and curl surface the edge of the mat up to face you. It is expected for the project to peel from the mat. And you can pull off the project by curling the mat up to make it easier in removing.

# Chapter 7

# MAINTENANCE OF CRICUT EXPLORE AIR 2

## HOW TO RESET CRICUT EXPLORE AIR 2

To resolve some Cricut Explore Air 2 machine faults that may include machine freezes, power problems, cutting issues, and behavior that seems not typical to the machine. Resetting the machine is a better way to start the troubleshooting step. The following steps will resolve most of the problems that your Cricut machine may encounter.

**Steps:**

1. Turn On your Cricut machine and make sure that the cartridge is not loaded.

2. Next is to roll your gray dials down and ensure they are at the lowest setting.

3. Then hold the cylinder blade assembly (green/gold) and use it to haul the whole gray carriage car unit along the track to the other side.

4. Press a red button in the gray carriage and wait for 2 to 3 seconds.

5. Allow it to go and then shift the gray carriage into its place.

6. The next is to roll all the dials way up and way down three times for each dial.

7. Then press the Cut button and turn Off the Cricut machine.

8. Allow the machine to rest for 15 to 20 seconds.

9. Then load the cartridge," On" the machine and practice a cut.

## HOW TO CHANGE BLADES IN THE CRICUT EXPLORE AIR 2

This information will tell you time to change your blade in the Cricut Explore Air 2:

1. When you are having issues weeding the projects due to cut lines.

2. When you were always changing the default pressure to more when on multiple projects.

3. When you set the proper settings, but the machine is not cutting the material thoroughly.

4. When you discovered that your machine is no longer cutting intricate designs again.

## HOW OFTEN SHOULD THE BLADE BE CHANGED?

1. Depending on how often you use the Cricut machine.

2. Depending on the types of material you are cutting on the machine.

## HOW TO CHANGE BLADE IN THE CRICUT EXPLORE AIR 2

**Steps:**

In the Cricut Explore Air 2, you will notice that there are two clamps;

Clamp A: This is for pens or other accessories.

Clamp B: This is for the blade.

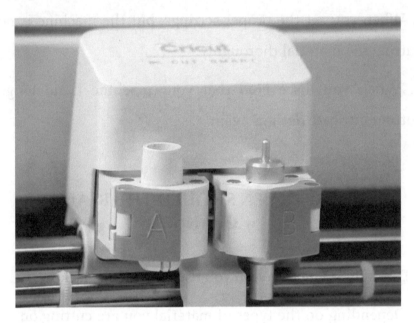

**Clamp A & B**

1. Open clamp B in the Cricut Explore Air 2

2. Pull up the whole housing of the blade and remove it from the clamp.

3. Push down the plunger of the blade housing. This act will push the blade out and then remove the blade carefully from the housing.

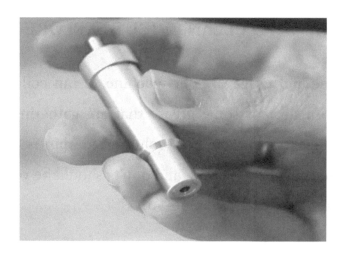

**Push the plunger**

4. Depending on the blade's condition, at times, you just need to clean the blade. Or you may need to replace the blade.

5. To replace the blade, carefully remove the protective cover from the new blade and then enter the blade shaft into the housing and the magnet inside will hold it in place.

Image shaft into the housing

6. Return the housing into the clamp B, ensure the top of the housing is flushed with the clamp's top, and then close.

# HOW TO CLEAN CRICUT EXPLORE AIR 2

With time and usage of your machine, it can collect paper particles or dust or some grease that are gathering around the carriage track. The best solution to this is cleaning. However, the following do's, and don'ts should be your guide to cleaning your Cricut Explore Air 2.

**Do's:**

1. Make sure that you turn off your machine if you want to start cleaning.

2. To clean, use a non-alcohol baby wipe to clean the machine.

3. Use the baby wipe to clean the rollers to get rid of residue.

4. Clean the blade housing to get rid of the dust and residue.

5. You may remove the housing to be able to clean the housing very well.

**Don'ts":**

1. Don't spray the cleaner directly on the Cricut machine.

2. It would be best if you did not clean off the grease on the bar holding the housing as it must be there.

3. Do not touch the gear chain at the back of the machine.

4. Avoid cleaning while the machine is On.

# HOW TO GREASE CRICUT EXPLORE AIR 2

The following steps are necessary to grease your machine to aid its productivity.

**Steps:**

1. Ensure to turn Off your machine.

2. Turn the Cut Smart carriage slowly until it moves to the left.

3. Use the non-alcohol baby wipe to clean its bar (entire bar).

4. Turn it again until it moves to the right.

5. Redo the process of cleaning the carriage with a wipe and the entire bar.

6. Move it to the center.

7. Open the machine lubrication packet and put a small amount of grease till the end of the cotton swab.

8. Apply small grease to both sides of the Cut Smart carriage and around the bar and into both sides of the carriage.

9. Move the Cut Smart carriage slowly to the left and then to the right to pass the grease evenly along the entire bar.

10. Remove the excess grease that is built up at the ends of the bar.

# HOW TO CLEAN CUTTING MATS

It is the level of the dirtiness of your machine that will determine the cleaning you will select in the list of below:

## Using Baby Wipes to clean Cricut Machine Mat

To clean your machine, you can make use of alcohol-free baby wipes and fragrance.

**Steps:**

1. Wipe the mat from top to bottom with the baby wipes.

2. If the mat is too dirty, rinse it under warm water.

3. Use a paper towel to pat dry it.

4. Allow the mat to dry.

## Using Soap and Water

For this method, it is recommended to use dish soap as harsh chemicals in the soap will damage the adhesive on the mat. Please don't use a brush, but a scrapper or a cloth to clean it.

**Steps:**

1. Pour warm water on the cutting mat.

2. Pour dish soap and scrub gently in a circular movement with a cloth.

3. Use water to remove the remaining soap on the mat.

4. Use a paper towel to pat dry it.

5. Allow drying with the surrounding air.

Note: Don't use a bath towel to dry it.

## Recoating the mat with New Adhesive

If you discovered that your cutting mat had lost its stickiness, you could make it alive again by re-coating it with new adhesive.

There are so many products you can make use that will do the job, such as glue stick and spray adhesive.

**Steps:**

1. Get alcohol and use it to get rid of any remaining adhesive.

2. Use painter's tape to cover the edges of the mat to protect it from the adhesive.

3. Spray the product evenly.

4. Allow the spray to dry by air.

5. Once it is dry, remove the painter's tape.

**How to make your Mat last longer**
The first rule is to keep your mat with its protective cover, and the remaining rules are below;

1. Run your lint roller on the mat to get rid of threads and lint.

2. Immediately get rid of debris and dirt after use.

3. Avoid using any harsh chemicals when cleaning the mat.

5. Don't touch the mat with your hands.

6. Try not to scrap the mat when you want to remove materials from the mat.

7. Gently clean the mat so as not to remove the adhesive.

8. Don't bend the cutting mat so as not to snap and break.

## How to make Cutting Mat Sticky

The main reason why your mat must be sticky is for your materials not to slide down when the machine is cutting. You will discover that initially your Cricut mats were sticking very well and still sticky for a couple of cuts. Later you realized that the mat is becoming less sticky or not sticky again. So to solve the issue of not sticking, you decide to make the mat sticky also. Since you don't want to waste materials and jamming of your machine every time.

Cutting mats are expensive as they are made from rubber that's why they are tacky.

So before you decide to make your cutting mat sticky again, the first is to clean the mat as described earlier.

As said earlier, the first step is to clean your cutting mat very well, and then you follow the next steps.

**Steps:**

1. Rub alcohol on the surface of the original layer of the cutting mat to remove it. Or you can use a scraper to remove the original surface from the cutting mat.

2. Get rid of the stickiness from the edges of the mat by masking painter's tape off the edges. Make sure that the tips are not sticky with the adhesive so as not to destroy the rollers.

3. Cover the mat with an adhesive to restore the stickiness. There are different kinds of adhesive, some are sprays, and some can be brushed.

4. Allow the cutting to air dry, get rid of the tape, and your mat is ready to be used.

Note: So remember that to make your mat last longer, you be always clean your mat.

# Chapter 8

# TROUBLESHOOTING CRICUT EXPLORE AIR 2

### The solution to Button Blinking Red

Note: Make sure to know the time when the power button starts to blink or flash red, and select the appropriate troubleshooting below:

### When you are powering the Machine:

If the button starts to blink or flash the moment you start the machine. It is recommended to get to the Member Care for further assistance.

### When you are updating firmware:

If the button starts to blink or flash the moment you want to update the machine firmware. It is recommended to get to the Member Care for further assistance.

**When you are loading mat:**

If the button starts to blink or flash when you want to load cutting, adhere to the following steps:

1. If you are having an issue with multiple projects.

If the issue is only for one project, the problems may have happened due to saving a corrupted project. The solution is to recreate the project with the situation.

If the issue persists, go to the next step 2.

2. It is possible that the roller bars may have been covered with dust that may be the source of the error. The next is to off the machine and remove the carriage car across the roller bar manually to be able to clean the specks of dust.

3. If the issue persists, contact the Member Care for assistance.

**Issues when you are cutting a project**

This happens when the blade, material, or mat is stuck in the material.

Steps:

1. Do all your materials stuck?

If it happens, it is an indication of a machine problem. Turn off the machine, then move the carriage car front and back for more than five times. Then on the machine, attempt the project again.

If the issue persists, get across to the Member Care for further assistance.

2. Do you use Knife Blade?

The knife Blade is designed in such a way to cut leather and balsa wood materials. The machine is designed to blind red light when never the blade is stuck in it.

Simply follow the instruction on the screen, clear the dirt's, and press the power button again, and it should resume cutting also.

3. If the problem persists, get across to the Member Care for assistance.


**Cricut Machine fails to cut through material**

If you discover that your Cricut machine is not cutting through your material or is just scoring the material. The following troubleshooting should help you in resolving the issue.

**Steps:**

1. Ensure that the material settings you select in Design Space or on the Smart Set Dial are compatible with the machine mat's material.

2. Open the Clamp and gently remove the blade housing from the machine. Don't use any other blade apart from the Cricut brands. The next is to check both the blade and housing to remove dust that has stocked or logged. After cleaned, attempt to test if the blade and its housing are now in good condition. If the issue persists, go to step 3.

3. Next, open the Manage Custom Materials page on the account menu and increase the pressure for the material setting using 2 to 4. Then try a test cut.

4. Try to cut another material like printer paper with the appropriate setting for it. If you do not experience the same result, then the issue is the material you want to cut.

5. Simply open your browser and clear cookies and cache, then try to test cut. If the issue persists, use another browser.

6. If all the above steps failed, then contact Member Care for assistance.

**If the Cricut machine is dragging or tearing the material**

There are many reasons that may lead to the issues raised above. If either of your machines is dragging or tearing material, follow the steps below to be able to resolve it.

Steps:

1. It is recommended that you have to select the appropriate material setting in Design Space, or your Smart Set Dial is set at correct settings. And make sure that when you are using a Custom setting, the material must be the right material to be selected from the drop-down list.

2. Check the size and how the image is if you want to cut an image which is either delicate or small. It is a recommendation to cut the image in a simple way or a small way.

Note that if changing to cutting in a simple image solves the problem, attempt to cut the delicate image with the aid of Custom setting for Cardstock.

3. Gently remove the blade housing from the machine, and remove the specks of dust gathered in the housing or blade.

4. Lower the pressure settings for the particular material in the Manage Custom Materials by increase 2 to 4. You can get to the Manage Custom Material via your account menu and choose Edit Custom Material on your Mat Preview screen after pressing Change Material (You may need to do this 3 to 5 times before you can see results).

5. Try to cut another material like copy paper in its appropriate setting. The problem may be with the material that has an issue.

6. Get and use a new blade and mat.

7. If the issue persists, get across to the Member Care.

If your machine is making an unusual noise.

If you discovered that your machine is having unusual noise, follow these steps to resolve the issue.

**If it is Grinding Noise**
**Steps:**

1. When you push the cut button of your machine, and the carriage car makes an unusual noise, it is advisee to record a video on how the machine is making noise and send it to the

Member Care.

2. If you buy a new machine and upon the first set up, it makes an unusual noise, it is advised to get across to the Member Care for further assistance. But if you are having been using the machine and it just starts to make a loud noise, follow the next step.

3. It is appropriate for you to use the power card cord that comes with the machine package. Using another brand may lead to the machine having the wrong voltage that will lead to a grinding noise? But if you are having the same issue with the Cricut power cord, go to the next step.

4. Check your pressure setting if it is not too high. Lower the pressure settings for the particular material in the Manage Custom Materials by an increase of 2 to 4. You can get to the Manage Custom Material via your account menu and choose Edit Custom Material on your Mat Preview screen after pressing Change Material (You may need to do this 2 to 3 times before you can see results).

5. If the issue persists, get across to the Member Care for assistance.

**Loud Noise**

• If your machine is having noise louder than standard, check if you engage fast Mode for cutting or writing. But if not, get across to the Member care for assistance.

• Cut sensor light does fail to turn on while Print Then Cut

• If the cut sensor light on your machine does not turn on when you want to engage in Print, then Cut projects, you are advised to follow these steps:

**Cricut Explore**

**Steps:**

1. Off the power of your machine.

2. Press on A and B Clamps immediately till the sensor light comes up. The next is to release the clamps, and the machine will turn on. Try to cut the image to check if it has been resolved.

3. But if the light does not come on after the previous step, get across to the Member Care for assistance.

**Cricut maker**

**Steps:**

1. Off the power of your machine.

2. Press on A and B Clamps immediately till the sensor light comes up. The next is to release the clamps, and the machine will turn on. Try to cut the image to check if it has been resolved.

3. But if after the previous step, the light does not come on, get across to the Member Care for assistance.

The light on the Carriage is turning off and on unexpectedly

The duty of the cut sensor light on the carriage to scan cut sensor marks on Print Then Cut projects.

Note that if there is no such issue during the cut-only project, it is okay, and if it is during the cut-only projects, it's also okay.

When you are on your machine and the issue surfaces, it means that either one or both of the clamps is in the down position. Shut the machine off and lift the clamps and On the machine.

If, after the previous step, there is no solution, contact the

Member Care for assistance.

## Mat is crooked when loaded into the Machine

There are some reasons why you may encounter such feats. The following steps are ways to resolve it.

**Steps:**

1. Check if the roller is loose, uneven, or damaged. If it encountered any of the problems mentioned above, take a picture of it and send it to the Member Care. But if it is not loose, uneven, or damaged, then go to the next step.

2. Check if you are using the right mat size for the Cricut machine. If the size is correct and you are still having the same issue, go to the next step.

3. Make sure that the mat is placed in line with the guides on your machine. If the mat is placed well and the issue continues, go to the next step.

4. Gently push the mat under the roller as the machine is about to start.

5. If all the above steps failed to contact the member Care for assistance.

# Chapter 9

# FAQS ON CRICUT EXPLORE AIR 2

### What software must I install for Cricut Explore Air 2?

The main software that compliments your machine is Design Space. To download the software, launch design.cricut.com with your browser on the computer and log in with your Cricut Id. If you are a first-timer, you will be directed to download Design Space software and be guided on installing the machine.

If you are on iOS or Android mobile device, search for the Design Space app on Google Play (Android) or App Store (iOS) and download the Cricut Design Space App. After this, simply sign in with your Cricut ID.

### What are the weight and dimensions of the Cricut Explore Air 2?

Weight: 9.5Kg (21 lbs.)

Length: 22.17" (563.3mm)

Height: 5.97" (151.59mm)

Width: 6.99" (177.57mm)

**How to connect Cricut Explore Air 2 to the computer?**

You have two options to connect your Cricut machine to the computer; either connect through USB cable or via Bluetooth.

**Is Wireless Bluetooth Adapter necessary for the Cricut Explore Air 2?**

Your Cricut Explore Air 2 comes with in-built Bluetooth, so you don't need a Wireless Bluetooth Adapter. However, if your computer does not Bluetooth, then get the Bluetooth dongle from the store.

**How to connect Cricut Explore Air 2 to the computer through Bluetooth?**

The first is to turn On your Cricut Explore and search for Bluetooth settings on your computer and get the device. The next is to pair the machine and the computer. But in case it asks of a password, enter 0000.

**How easy is it to use Cricut Explore Air 2?**

Using Cricut Explore Air 2 is very easy and straightforward.

## What are the main features of Cricut Explore Air 2?

Cricut Explore Air 2 affords you the easy way to curve. It comes with a smart dial set for the parameter of the materials to cut. It also has a double tool holder, and print then cut option with a scoring stylus. With the aid of Design Space, you have the chance to create projects with all types of materials that include poster board and cardstock.

## How many materials can Cricut Explore Air 2 cut with the help of Cricut Access?

With Cricut Access, you can make use of over 100 different materials. Check the Cricut Access to know the types of materials you can use.

## What is the smart set dial for Cricut Explore Air 2?

Your machine comes with a smart set dial. This smart set dial will help you select the proper settings with the material you want to work on. Remember that once you have set the dial, it will be there unless you change it.

## Can Cricut Explore Air 2 cut vinyl?

Yes. Your Cricut Explore Air 2 will do this with ease. And don't forget that Cricut Explore Air 2 is 2x faster than other

Cricut machines.

**Is it possible to use my machine without a subscription?**

Yes. You can use it for free in the Design Space. But if you want to access the Cricut library for fonts, images and ready to use projects, you will have to pay for Cricut Access.

# Chapter 10

# SIMPLE PROJECTS ON THE CRICUT EXPLORE AIR 2

## MAKING SIMPLE HANDMADE CARDS

**Materials Needed:**

Cricut Explore Air 2 machine

Fine Point Blade

Cricut cardstock

Corrugated Paper

Home Printer

Cricut Pen (Black)

Light and StandardGrip Mat

Cricut Scoring Stylus

**Steps:**

1. Launch your design.cricut.com and design the graphics that you desired.

2. Use your preferred shape to create how you want your card to look like.

3. Add the kind of text you want on your card that will bring out the beauty you desired.

4. When you are done with attaching all the objects, now click on Make It.

5. The mat preview will display how and where to put your design on the mat before been printed.

6. There is a tiny mat preview that tells you the next step on the left side after project copies.

7. Click Continue, and you will be directed step by step before you embark on cutting.

8. When you click on Send to Printer, it will send the project to the home printer. Ensure that your printer is connected to the computer.

9. Click Print.

10. On your machine, choose the type of material you want to print.

11. Next is to load the mats and tools.

If you are scoring and cutting the project, you must have a Cricut pen, fine point blade, and scoring stylus.

12. Click Press.

# MAKING A SIMPLE T-SHIRT WITH IRON-ON VINYL

**Materials Needed:**

Cricut Explore Air 2 machine

Cricut Easypress 2

Cricut Easypress Mat

Jersey shirt (100% cotton)

Weeding Tool

Standard Mat

Vinyl

Brayer Tool

Scissors

**Steps:**

1. Launch your design.cricut.com with your Cricut ID on your device and create your design, or you can use any of the ready to use projects. If this is your first time using iron-on vinyl to customize a shirt, it is advised to choose an easy and

straightforward design to print and cut on your Cricut machine.

2. Check your Design Space to confirm if your jersey shirt's color is the same as shown on your canvas. If not, check the right-hand side of your screen, click on the canvas, and then change the canvas's color to your shirt's color.

3. Save the project with the color on your Design Space and name it.

4. Once you have saved your project, a green Cricut symbol in the Design Space will appear. Tap this button to begin the process of cutting your custom shirt using iron-on vinyl. There will display a cutting mat on the screen. Choose the correct cutting mat size for your design to fit appropriately within the cutting mat.

5. Before you begin cutting, make sure your material is loaded rightly in the Cricut Explore Air 2. You are to place the liner face down when making use of iron-on vinyl. Once you have done the right thing, click Cut on your device screen.

6. Both the Design Space and the Cricut machine will blink to indicate that the material dial set is appropriately set.

Once you have loaded the material and set the correct dial set, the Cricut Explore Air 2 will blink, and the machine is ready to cut.

7. Click on Hit on the Cricut button on the Cricut Explore Air 2, and the magic will start.

8. Once the project is cut, remove the excess part of the iron-on vinyl and leave the right part on the cutting mat.

9. Use the weeding tool to get rid of any design pieces that are not part of the final project.

10. Set the Easypress mini 2 to linen or cotton setting to achieve the best result when using iron-on vinyl on the shirt.

11. Place the shirt's design and use your Easypress mini to heat the vinyl for the design to stick. This should be between 15 to 35 seconds.

# MAKING LEATHER EARRINGS FOR JEWELRY

**Materials Needed:**

Cricut Explore Air 2

Deep Cut Blade

Cricut Transfer Tape

Strong Grip Mat

Scrap Leather

Leather Earrings Template Cut File

Jewelry Pliers

Awl

Earring Hooks

**Steps:**

1. It will be better if you can use scrap leather instead of getting new leather. Get your preferred color for this project.

2. Trim your piece of leather to be the size of earrings you want. Also, you have to cut a piece of transfer tape with the same size as that of the piece of leather for earrings.

3. Place the leather squarely on the peeled transfer tape and let the base of the leather touching the sticky side of the tape—this helps in keeping your cutting mat from debris.

4. Install your blade into the Cricut machine, turn the dial to custom, and select leather from the Design Space drop-down list screen.

5. Cut the leather with your machine.

6. Once the leather is cut, peel the cutting mat and remove the tape from the leather's back.

7. If the cutting is not perfect, take the scissor to trim to your desired design.

8. Create a small hole at the top of the earrings.

9. Use the pliers to place the hooks into the earrings.

# MAKING A VINYL STICKER

**Materials Needed:**

Cricut Explore Air 2 machine

Transfer Tape

Vinyl

Cutting mat

Weeding tool

Scrapper

**Steps:**

1. Launch your design.cricut.com and create your design, or you can use any ready to use projects.

2. Place the vinyl on the cutting mat with the paper liners side close to the mat.

3. Load the cutting mat into the Cricut Explore Air 2 and set the smart set dial to Vinyl. This indicates that your machine is set to cut vinyl material.

4. Hit Go.

5. Once the cut is complete, remove the vinyl from the mat.

6. Use your weeding tool to remove the unwanted vinyl on the design.

7. Where you want the vinyl to be placed, simply clean and dry the area thoroughly.

8. Mark where you want to put the design.

9. Cut transfer tape that is the same as your design.

10. Get rid of the liner from the transfer tape.

11. Let both the design and the tap aligned.

12. The next step is to peel the liner from the vinyl design. The transfer tape will hold the vinyl in place.

13. Now, place the sticker to where you want to use it.

14. Press down the sticker firmly from the center to the edges.

15. Then, carefully remove the transfer tape from the surface of the sticker.

# HOW TO USE VINYL ON PAINTED WOOD

**Materials Needed:**

Cricut Explore Air 2 machine

Adhesive vinyl (black)

Weeding tool

Adhesive vinyl (pink)

Scrapper

Transfer tape

Wood sign

Paintbrush

White paint

**Steps:**

1. You will have to paint your wood if it is raw. And if the surface of the wood is rough, you will need to sand it well, as the better, it is smooth, the better the vinyl will stick on it.

2. When the wood is very smooth, then paint it well. I suggest you use acrylic paint.

3. Allow the wood to dry well.

4. Go to your Design Space platform and create your design.

5. Make sure your design's size is the same as the size of the painted wood. Use the size tool in the Edit Toolbar to resize the image if it not the same with the wood size.

6. Once the sizes are the same, then click on Make It on your screen. You will be directed to cut the vinyl. You do not need to mirror as it is not iron-on vinyl. Place the vinyl side up on the mat. Place the mat into the Cricut machine and tap the blinking C to effect the cutting.

7. Once the project is cut, use the weeding tool to remove the unwanted vinyl.

8. Place the cut vinyl face upward and place the transfer tape on it.

9. Use the scrapper to stick the vinyl to the transfer tape.

10. Put the vinyl and the transfer tape on the project and stick it well to the wood.

11. The next is to remove the transfer tape.

# USING INFUSIBLE INK ON BAG

**Materials Needed:**

Cricut Explore Air 2

Cricut Infusible Ink transfer Sheet

Green StandardGrip Cricut Mat

Cricut Infusible Ink Blank Bag

Cricut Easypress Mini 2

Easypress 2 Mat

Weeding Tool

Cardstock

Lint Roller

Butcher Paper

Heat-resistance tape

**Steps:**

1. Go to Design Space and create a beautiful design or artwork for your bag.

2. Resize the design to fit the size of the surface of your bag.

3. Ensure to mirror the artwork, as infusible ink is similar to iron-on vinyl, and the image must be reversed; after this, click Continue.

4. Choose Infusible Transfer Sheet in the make screen as your material.

5. Insert the Fine Point blade into the Cricut machine.

6. Place the infusible ink transfer sheet liner face down on the green cutting mat. Insert into the Cricut Explore Air 2 and cut.

7. Use your weeding tool to weed out the unwanted part of the graphics.

8. Now insert the Easypress mat into the bag with cardstock on top of it.

9. Use the lint roller to get rid of any dust that maybe with the bag.

10. Cover the bag with the butcher paper and preheat the bag to help flatten the surface and dry the moisture.

11. Press the Easypress at 400C iron for 15 seconds on the bag and allow it to cool completely.

12. Immediately, the bag is cooled, place the project on the surface cooled.

13. Then put the butcher paper on the project. Carefully place the Easypress on it and press for 40 seconds.

14. Allow the transfer cool, and it will stick on the bag.

# CUSTOMIZED VINYL MUG

**Materials Needed:**

Cricut Explore Air 2 machine

White Mug

Permanent Vinyl (3 colors)

Weeding tool

Blue Cutting Mat

Transfer tape

**Steps:**

1. Go to Design Space and create your artwork or you can download the SVG file from the website and upload it into your canvas.

2. Resize the artwork to the size of the surface of the mug.

3. The next is to cut the project. You don't need to mirror regular adhesive vinyl.

4. Use your weeding tool to remove the negative part of the material of the project.

5. Cut the size of the transfer tape that is equal to the size of the design.

6. Remove the paper at the back of the transfer tape and place it over the design.

7. Make sure that you burnish the tape very to the vinyl.

8. Remove, and the design will stick to the transfer tape.

9. Place the transfer on the mug from the middle to everywhere until it pressed well to the mug.

Chapter 11

# HOW TO MAKE MONEY WITH YOUR CRICUT EXPLORE AIR 2

Several people have been asking questions if it is possible to make money with Cricut Explore Air 2.

The absolute answer is YES; you can! There are tons of people that are making cool cash with their Cricut machines.

Do you realize that getting things done with the internet is now more accessible than before, and coupled with huge users online every day? Even with the outstanding statistic of people making money online, there are still enormous opportunities to make money with your crafts locally.

What will determine the amount of money you will be making is mostly dependent on what you will be selling, marketing, time and money you invest in the business.

## How to make money with the Cricut machine?

The primary way to make money with your Cricut machine is to create personalized products for customers that want and need them. The Cricut Explore Air 2 and other families of Cricut machines can cut many types of materials. So using them to create items and crafts for people will be an excellent way to make money.

Another way to make your knowledge about the Cricut machines scalable is to teach other people how to master the Cricut machine from a beginner's level to the advanced level. No wonder if you check the internet, you will find several stores and individuals having paid classes both offline and online for people who want to learn how to become a master in the usage of Cricut machines and a way to monetize the knowledge gained.

You can also make money with your knowledge about Cricut by blogging and uploading your crafting videos on Youtube. You will be surprised at the number of people looking for instructions and projects on Cricut when you go on Google or Youtube.

There are so many free and inexpensive resources on the internet where you will learn about this Cricut Crafts if you decide to thread this business path.

**Which of the Cricut Machine is the best?**

People are asking which of the Cricut machines the best in the crafting business is. My candid answer is first to get the one you can afford, and later when you are making money, get the one that can do what the one you purchased could not do.

I will suggest that if you can afford it, it is advised to buy Cricut Explore Air 2 and Cricut Maker. We will discuss below why these are excellent when it comes to crafting.

The Cricut Explore Air 2 can cut different kinds of materials that include vinyl. Another advantage of this machine is that it can cut 2x faster when you are creating bulk items.

The Cricut Maker comes with many more advantages than other Cricut machines as it can cut thick materials, sew projects and comes with various blades and accessories that will make its job more comfortable to do.

**Next Step:**

After you have gotten your machine and know crafting on the machine, the next step is to have a business plan of what to be done.

Now, if you intend to customize t-shirts, you will need to have iron-on vinyl, Infusible Ink, jersey shirts, and many others. Since you have decided on iron-on vinyl as your material, you will need a heat press. Though there are traditional heat transfers, the best that will give you the best result due to heat transfer, especially when you are on mass production, is Cricut EasyPress mini 2.

**Design Step:**

If you are a graphic designer, you may not have much problem in this regard, but if you are a novice when it comes to design, it is better to go to some websites that we offered earlier in this book and download the graphics that you will be using for your projects.

If you are a designer or want to learn design, I recommend that you go online and sample some project ideas and tweak it to make it personal.

At this stage, if you are not motivated, you may drop by the roadside. This stage of designing your artworks requires perseverance, patience, and motivation to succeed.

## Will the business be Online or Offline?

The next step is to decide if you want your business to be offline or online. With the internet's presence, I advise people to get a website to make your business travel faster. And there are places where you can get cheap domain and hosting.

## Where to sell my products?

There are many places online and offline where you can sell your products, and some are below;

**Etsy:** This is the most popular site to get customers who will buy your products without a website.

**Facebook groups:** Join Facebook groups that are into what you are doing. Familiarize yourself with other members of the groups so it will not look as if you are spamming the groups. Ask for permission from the admins to know if you can post your products in the groups. But it is better to join your local groups in your area on Facebook.

**Personal Websites.** Getting a domain name and hosting is cheap. What could be the major challenge is the development of the site. With little money, you will get a website developer who is a freelancer in some online markets.

**Craft Fairs:** Check your local Facebook groups, school bulletins, Nextdoor, newsletter, and others to know when there will be other craft fairs or events in your area.

**Social Media:** Create an account with Facebook, Instagram, Twitter, and other social media to expose your business.

**Personal Hosting:** Create your function and invite people to your home to see your products.

**Charity Events:** Go to charity events and donate charities and raffles that will be converted to your products.

**Family and friends:** Don't be shy of your passion. Tell friends and family about your crafts. You will be amazed at how some of them will support you in marketing your products.

**What about the time?**

You may invest more time in the beginning, but once you are

an expert in the game, you become a master, and you will use little time to come out with excellent products.

**Where to purchase material?**

There are many places to buy your materials. The best is to get your materials from reputable sources. There are lots of them out there, but we will recommend that you check their reviews before you start purchasing from them. The best place to buy is no other place than the cricut.com itself.

Other places are;

Amazon

Walmart

Craft Chameleon

Primary.com

Jiffy Shirts

Joann Fabrics

JPIblanks.com

Standoutvinyl.com

And lots more.

Ensure to check local stores in your area.

**Projects to embark on?**

There is no limit to what you can make with your Cricut machines. Don't limit your ideas. Simply go outside the box. Go to Esty.com and check the trending products, but don't copy out rightly as it will lead to copyright issues.

Project Ideas:

Personalized gifts

Custom tote bags

Water bottles

Floral arrangements

T-shirts

Signs

Backpacks

Personalized Clothing

Papercraft

School designs and initials

BowPainted wood signs

Tea towels

Lunchboxes

Potholders

Toys

Earrings

Bracelets

Ornaments

Tumbler

Card sets

**Some of the materials needed for this business:**

Wood

Iron-On Vinyl

Felt

Leather

Cardstock

Aluminum

**How do I charge my products?**

This question is tough to answer. But there is standard advice on how to charge, and this is what we will recommend.

Multiply the cost of your material by three, that's the selling price. If your vinyl costs $3, then you will sell it for $9.

To be successful in this business, there are some tips we will recommend and are;

1. Don't just start any project. Make sure the projects are feasible and will not take much of your time.

2. Research very well on your target area before you commence the business.

3. Be perfect in one area before you jump to another area.

4. Be organized in your work.

5. Keep financial records.

We wish you the best of luck in your endeavor.

# CONCLUSION

Thank you for Purchasing this Guide!

The Cricut Explore Air 2 is a machine to be bought if you a lover of crafts, as it is the wonder of the Cricut family.

If you don't know how to use Cricut Explore Air 2 machine quickly and straightforward, this book presents them. You are under-utilizing your Cricut machine. Not only is this book for Cricut Explore Air 2 only, but it also covers how to master Design Space and how to make money with your Cricut machine.

Once you master how to use Cricut Explore Air 2 with the Design Space platform and how to turn Cricut Explore Air 2 into a cash machine, the sky is the limit for Cricut designs and projects.

If you found this guide helpful, do not hesitate to send it to your friends who love homemade crafts or share it with them. Not only are you encouraging them, but you are also supporting my work.

Thanks

.

# Reference:

https://help.cricut.com/hc/en-us/articles

http://www.craftedge.com/support/cricut/cricut_reset.html

https://personaldiecutting.com/how-to-link-cartridges-with-the-cricut-explore/

Tiffany Nicholas: Cricut Design Space: Beginner's Guide To Mastering The Design Space & Cricut Machines with ScreenShots, Illustrations, and Project Ideas

Made in United States
Troutdale, OR
05/12/2025

31290602R00159